Thanuja

Praise for the Book

'*Thanuja: A Memoir of Transition and Migration* is a free expression of emotions and experiences. I read this book from cover to cover without putting it down. It expresses truths that have never been expressed before without concealing anything. I would like to thank Shobhasakti for publishing this book first in Tamil. Thanuja had come all the way from Germany to meet me at the JLF literary festival in 2016 in London. I could see the impact that my autobiography *The Truth about Me: A Hijra Life Story* had had on her. As a writer I am glad that my autobiography has had the same impact on Thanuja that Bama's autobiography *Karukku* had in inspiring me to write. My heartfelt congratulations to Thanuja! I believe Thanuja's ability to overcome the exploitation that she had to suffer in the name of love, her determination not to succumb to her suicidal thoughts and her success as an established dental hygienist will be an inspiration to the many heartbroken and suicidal transwomen who are alive today. I am proud of Thanuja for her determination to advance in life without being disillusioned by the oppression, ostracisation and violence that she has suffered.'

A. Revathi, author of *The Truth about Me: A Hijra Life Story*

Thanuja

A Memoir of Migration and Transition

Thanuja Singam

Translated by Kiran Keshavamurthy

BLOOMSBURY
NEW DELHI • LONDON • OXFORD • NEW YORK • SYDNEY

BLOOMSBURY INDIA
Bloomsbury Publishing India Pvt. Ltd
Second Floor, LSC Building No. 4, DDA Complex, Pocket C – 6 & 7,
Vasant Kunj, New Delhi, 110070

BLOOMSBURY, BLOOMSBURY INDIA and the Diana logo
are trademarks of Bloomsbury Publishing Plc

First published in Tamil as *Thanuja* by Karuppu Piradhigal, 2020, and edited by Shobasakthi
This edition published 2024

ISBN: PB: 978-93-56407-32-9; eBook: 978 93 56408 10 4
2 4 6 8 10 9 7 5 3 1

Typeset in Bembo Std by Manipal Technologies Limited
Printed and bound in India by Thomson Press India Ltd

MIX
Paper | Supporting responsible forestry
FSC® C010615

To all the transgender people in the world
and
to Arnab, with love and gratitude

Kiran Keshavamurthy

Contents

Preface xi

Part I 1

1. The War 3
2. A Thousand Fireflies 5
3. In Praise of Madurai 8
4. Appa's Return 10
5. The First Sacrifice 13
6. Beautiful Chennai 16
7. First Love 18
8. Colombo 22
9. Amma's Arrival 27
10. Sexual Violence 28
11. Yazhpanam 30
12. Willkommen 34
13. World Wide Web 38
14. Forest Dwellers and Hip Hop 42
15. Thirty Pills 46
16. A Search for My Own Gender Identity 47
17. The Magical Device 53
18. A New School 55
19. Kirsten and Murat 58
20. The Thief's Lover 61
21. The Magic of Hormones 65
22. The Brothers 68
23. A Meeting of Transwomen 72
24. The New Amma 77
25. Group Discussion 83

26. The Chariot Festival 88
27. Holland 91
28. The Fortune of being Married 95
29. My First Glass of Alcohol 97
30. Love and War 99
31. I Knocked and the Doors Opened 102

Part II 107
32. The Holy Nirvanam 109
33. Kamini Chithi 114
34. Manjal Neerattu 116
35. The One Night Stand 120
36. Ceaseless Struggle 121
37. Rohan 123
38. Towards Zurich 125
39. Guru Mona 128
40. The Disco and Tamil Men 130
41. Getting to Know Myself 131
42. The Star Actresses 135
43. An Independent House 137
44. The Gateway to Death 139
45. Ceaseless Misfortune 141
46. Rabeek 144
47. The Women of Jaffna 147
48. A Lover from the Movies 148
49. Thailand 151
50. Canada 153
51. The Sensational Hero 156
52. The Man of My Dreams 161
53. The Days in Paris 164
54. At My Mother-in-Law's 166
55. Beyond Sorrow 169
56. The Wedding Sari 172
57. Legally a Woman 173
58. The Oldest Profession 175

59. Iyer Savitri 177
60. Carnival 180
61. The Interview 182
62. Back to Switzerland 184
63. The Queen 186
64. The Cremation Ground 189
65. Back to Tamil Nadu 190
66. Mentors 193
67. The Motherland 196
68. Menstruation 199

Translator's Afterword 203
Translator's Acknowledgements 214
About the Author 215
About the Translator 216

Preface

I was born and raised as a boy named 'Thanujan'; my name is now Thanuja. I got rid of a letter in my name and chose the name 'Thanuja' just like how I got rid of an unwanted part of my body—my penis. But I did not choose my gender; it was something that nature bestowed upon me.

I'm now twenty-nine. I have been living in Germany since I was twelve. When you read this book you may realise that my heart is rooted in the Tamil land. Although I can speak and write in three languages, I wrote my autobiography in my mother tongue. Even this wasn't my choice; I believe it came naturally to me.

I was once an escort who lived in a luxurious hotel and earned up to a thousand euros a night; I'm now a medical student training to become a dental hygienist. This is certainly my choice.

I asked myself if I should be writing an autobiography when I'm just twenty-nine. But I think I have lived four or five lives in this short life. I have experienced the greatest of joys and sorrows. I have tasted blood, tears and semen to the point of exhaustion. I have travelled across the world and met all kinds of people.

I have the opportunity to be the first *thirunangai* from Eezham to publish her autobiography.[1] Like salt

1 The word thirunangai was coined by M. Karunanidhi, the former chief minister of Tamil Nadu, to refer to transwomen. The term is a composite word that comprises two parts: *thiru* – mister; and *nangai* – woman. The word was created to replace earlier terms such as *ali*, *pedi* and *aravani* that the transgender community thought were discriminatory.

from the sea that will always be used even if there are thousands of other wonders and fishes in the sea, there will always be something for others to learn from my life, won't there?

I wish to present before you the words that glow in my heart in all their nakedness. Some of you may be disgusted at what I have to say. But I believe that the light that emerges from an honest heart is brighter than the moon or a forest fire. It is with this belief that I began writing this book.

PART I

1. The War

I have been a refugee since birth. The Indian Army massacred thousands of our people and transformed our land into an open prison by the time they left Sri Lanka in 1990. I was born the following year. By then, a brutal conflict known as the 'Second Eezham War' had begun. The Sri Lankan army, navy and air force were carrying out a genocide. The army had imposed a blockade on the Tamil regions and destroyed them. Rifles were aimed at us from ships anchored at sea. Sri Lanka's warplanes dropped bombs on us as they flew past.

Our small village, Mankumban, was besieged by the army when I was still in my mother's womb. The army looted and set fire to homes and raped women. Some of my relatives perished in the subsequent massacres. Others disappeared. The army set fire to my house. Our belongings, documents and land deeds were charred.

Mankumban is located between Allaipitti and Velanai on the island of Leiden in the northern part of Sri Lanka. The city of Yazhpanam is five kilometres away. The village is full of sandy hills. Most of the sand used to build the houses and buildings in Yazhpanam is from my village. At the foothills of these sandy hills is the seashore that glows like white marble and is popular among foreign tourists. Our village was not known for anything else—until the attack of the Sea Black Tiger, Angayarkanni, when I was three.

Angayarkanni's real name was Thuraisingam Puspakala. She lived very close to us. She had joined the Liberation Tigers Movement when she was young, becoming a 'Sea Black Tiger', one of the designated warrior cadres. When she was twenty-one, she attacked and destroyed the Sri Lankan navy commander's ship while it was anchored offshore in the Kankesanthurai Sea. My village became part of the history of the war because of Angayarkanni.

Our village is mostly Shaiva. There are a few Muslims and Christians too. But there has never been any communal conflict or violence. There were five Shiva temples in the village. At the edge of the village was the Satti Sinthathirai Matha temple. There was a mosque on the white seashore. I heard that there was a Shaiva man in my village who swept the mosque and kept it clean after the Tigers expelled Muslims from the village.

My family depended on the monsoons to farm their lands. There were no rivers or lakes in our village. I was the third child born to a poor family that survived on seasonal paddy, betel leaves and vegetables. My sister is seven years older and my brother is five years older than me.

Like thousands of other Tamil families, my family had to escape to India as refugees when the war intensified in December 1991. I was just three months old at the time, and my feet had never even touched the land where I was born, when we had to cross the choppy waves of the Palk Strait in a small boat.

In those days, if ten refugee boats left for India, only five would arrive safely. The other boats would either be captured by the Sri Lankan navy or capsize in the deep sea. My family somehow managed to flee to the shores of Rameswaram despite being subject to the Sri Lankan navy's intense surveillance and gunfire.

From there we went to Madurai. That city welcomed and embraced us. There were some refugee families from Eezham living in a place called

Kochadai in Madurai. Some of my relatives from Mankumban were there too. Our family went to Madurai in search of them. With their help, we could rent a house to live in.

But my family suffered because of the indifference of the Indian government and the financial difficulties we faced as refugees. My father, whom I called 'Appa', decided to go abroad to take care of the family's needs. He had relatives in Germany, and he planned to apply for asylum there. Once he was granted refuge, he would bring us to Germany.

Appa soon left for Germany and Amma was left alone with us three children. We often had to seek help from our refugee relatives who were scattered across Madurai. However, Appa soon began sending us money for our expenses and our lives grew peaceful.

My mother must have been happy that she could rescue her children from the brutal war. Her joy may have given her the strength to endure her husband's absence. When refugees escape a war-torn country, they don't just traverse land and water, they also traverse death.

2. A Thousand Fireflies

I had a very happy childhood. I did not have to face any of the obstacles that I would face later in life. When I was three, I felt an urge to wear my sister's clothes. I make no mistake when I say I was three. Everyone complimented my femininity. They thought it was some sort of a game.

My sister would help me dress and wear makeup. With my coy laughs, I would imitate Tamil actresses and video jockeys like Meena and Pepsi Uma. My performances would make everyone laugh. I never tired of watching cooking shows and beauty contests on television. I would comb and adorn my mother's hair and apply makeup to her face. My favourite toys were my Barbie doll and my small cooking dishes. I loved playing *pallanguzhi*.

People were right to call me a troublesome child. I was impertinent for my age; I argued with people and remembered everything that they said to me. I would talk to anyone who was passing by our house and walk with them to their homes. I did not think about where I was going or how I would return. I was not scared of getting lost. My mother would have to roam the streets in search of me.

When my mother could no longer put up with my nuisance, she tied one of my legs to a tree in front of our house. I was unable to free myself and had to beg my neighbours to untie me. I once swallowed my mother's pills and began vomiting. My mother had to rush me to the hospital. These were some of the many ways in which I troubled my mother.

I would accompany my mother to the temple every Friday. I would pray that God turn me into a woman. I did not know why I wished for this, but I believed that only God could transform someone who was born with a male body into a woman. But my wishes went beyond what God would do.

I spent most of my time alone on the terrace of our house. I would be lost in my own fantasy world in which I was transformed into a woman. That imaginary woman was very beautiful. She had very long hair. She was majestic. The secret joy that blossomed in my heart at that moment transported me into the night like thousands of fireflies.

I was admitted to school when I was five, but I never liked going to school. I went only because I was scared my mother would beat me if I didn't. My siblings and I went to Chandler Matriculation School, a reputed English-medium school in the city. But what difference did school make? I was not a good student. Despite all my efforts, people at school called me a fool.

There was a teacher named Saheela who often beat me because I never liked doing homework. She would hit me with a long bamboo stick. She would then call my brother and sister and complain to them about me. My brother would get upset and he would beat me too.

I was my sister's favourite. But she didn't like me being so talkative. Us siblings would take the school bus together. On the bus, I would sit among my sister's friends and tell them many stories. My boisterousness would irritate my sister, who was the embodiment of calmness. Her irritation would lead to strange punishments. One of them was to make me eat five hot green chillies.

I never won a quiz competition in school. I did not have the slightest faith in myself or in my intelligence. I was regularly thrashed at school, at home and at evening school. People firmly believed that they could turn a fool into an intelligent person by beating him. They perhaps thought that my tears would dissolve my foolishness.

Although she severely beat me, I admired Saheela. I love women who are majestic and proud. My teacher was such a woman. Even men would be intimidated by her. In my fantasy world on the terrace, I would imagine I was Saheela teaching imaginary students.

Early in the morning, my mother and I would draw *kolams*. I would wait for the milkman. I would place flowers before a picture of our God. Then I would help my mother cook. This behaviour didn't really bother my mother. She did not upset my imaginary world. In fact, she taught me how to cook and wash dishes.

I was openly celebrating my inner femininity. No one stopped me from adorning myself with my sister's clothes and my mother's jewellery. They thought I was just having fun.

3. In Praise of Madurai

My mother's cousin and her son lived nearby. My aunt's name is Raji. My aunt would come over in the evenings to watch television and chat with my mother. I was amazed at the ease with which my mother and aunt would wear saris. I never tired of watching them as they put on the garment. I would beg Raji to show me how to wear one too. She was the one who first taught me how to wear a sari.

Whenever I wore a sari, fireflies would transport me to my fantasy world. As I did not have long hair, I would tie a towel around my head and imagine it was my hair as I floated in my dreams. In Madurai, it was common for women who had come of age to wear *pavadai* and *davani*. I have always been fond of them because I have grown up watching women wear them.

Kochadai had dense groves and farms everywhere. I would run after grazing pigs. Sometimes, when the mother pig wasn't around, I would take one of the piglets in my arms and caress and kiss it. My mother disliked this behaviour and I would get beaten for it.

Though I was dull in school, I was an expert at stealing fruit from my neighbours' trees. I would climb the walls of their houses and pluck mangoes, guavas, coconuts and tamarind and eat them. Our house was on the banks of the Vaigai, and I would catch fish from the river and put them in our well. I would also catch crabs in the paddy fields.

Close to my house was the famous Kochadai Muthaiya temple. I would hide the slippers of those who visited the temple. The devotees would sacrifice a goat during a festival that was organised at the temple every year. Karakattam dancers would dance at the festival. I thought they were men dressed up as women. I was not old enough to know that they were transwomen like me. I was captivated by them and entranced by their sparkling skirts and ornaments. I thought I wanted to join a karakattam group when I grew up.

Other than studying, I was very happy at school. I would play kabaddi, cricket and badminton with my male friends. I would also play with my female friends. I did not discriminate between genders. I did what I liked doing. My school was Roman Catholic and it was there that I first discovered Jesus Christ. I was told of his miracles and began to love Jesus. I would chant and implore him to use his miraculous powers to turn me into a woman.

I love dancing. Mridangam, Bharatanatyam and Carnatic music were taught at school. Most of the male students would opt for mridangam. I learnt Bharatanatyam with the girls and also from watching Bharatanatyam performances on television. My dance performances were a part of the cultural programmes held at school and were very well received.

I had a very close friend named Mary. She was a very good student. She was the one who taught me how to ride a bicycle. We would attend Sunday school together. Mary and I were chosen to dance for Christmas at church. I dressed up as a woman for the performance.

Until then, I had only ever dressed up as a woman within the confines of my house. My mother, who had enjoyed watching me dress up as a girl when I was three, was no longer impressed. She began to shout at me for wearing female clothes indoors. But dancing in female clothes during Christmas was a golden opportunity to appear before the city in women's clothes. I did not want to miss this opportunity.

I told my mother, 'I'm going to dance for Jesus Christ.' She relented. I wore my sister's black pavadai and borrowed her earrings. I was worried that my hair was not long, but Mary did not have long hair either and that was somewhat comforting.

When I appeared on stage and began dancing, the audience thought I was a woman. When they praised me, I wished that I could wear these clothes for the rest of my life. But I knew that my mother would surely beat me if I went back home wearing them.

4. Appa's Return

In 1996, my father returned from Germany. Appa, who had left when I was a baby, was finally back in Madurai. He bought sketch pens, perfumes, clothes and sweets for us from Germany. Two of Appa's sisters came with him. Another sister visited from Sri Lanka along with my grandmother. That was when I discovered how big my family was. My aunts from Germany had come with their four children and my aunt from Sri Lanka had brought her five children along. My house was full of relatives.

My sister and brother were somewhat fair-complexioned. They would tease me for being dark-skinned. In Tamil families, children are consciously or unconsciously made to feel inferior because of their complexion. Tamils believe children who are born fair are beautiful and they humiliate children who have a darker complexion. My brother and sister would always tease me by saying that I was not born to our parents and had instead been discovered in a garbage bin. My mother too would say, 'Your father left because he disliked you for being dark.' I would believe what she said because that is how my father treated me.

I do not think my father had much love for me. He was a habitual drinker. Whenever he drank, he felt like beating someone. My sister would always be his first victim. I never liked seeing my father beating my sister. I once said '*Po da*!' to his face and ran away. After that, my father never beat her again. He would only beat me and my brother.

I could not spell my name without getting it wrong. It would make my father very angry. He would scold my mother by saying, 'You haven't raised him well.' Then he would thrash me. Once his anger had subsided, he would show me how to write my name in English and Tamil. I had to write my name every day without any spelling mistakes and show my father. But not once did I get it right. I was relieved when my father returned to Germany at the end of his holiday.

Three months after my father left, my sister came of age. It made me very happy and I too longed to reach sexual maturity. Menstruating women would hesitate to go to a shop to ask for sanitary napkins. They would ask boys like me to buy it for them. Whenever I bought sanitary napkins for my sister, I would insert one of them in my underwear and tell myself, 'I'm menstruating too.'

In our families, we organise grand coming-of-age ceremonies. The girl receives many new gifts including a new sari, jewellery and money during the ceremony. She is made to feel like a star. Most of the ceremony is spent with her posing for the videographer. The girl's maternal uncle (mama) has to buy her the first sari. Our mama lived in Canada but came to Madurai with his family for the ceremony. He had two sons. They did not know Tamil very well. I could not understand their Canadian English.

My mama pretended to be loving and concerned but he was a showoff. He kept talking about how amazing his life in Canada was. He never missed an opportunity to berate us siblings. He would compare his children to us and tell us how wonderful they were. Mama evoked my fascination with the West. I wished to talk like his sons and fly in planes. We kept pestering our mother to ask Appa to take us to Germany as soon as possible. She put up with our pestering with a smile.

My sister's ceremony went off well. My longing for a similar ceremony grew. I began to dream that someone was organising a coming-of-age ceremony for me. As the days went by, my effeminacy became a problem at home. My siblings did not like the fact that I wore female clothes and befriended women. They tormented me and warned me not to do it again. Those who were supposed to love me beat me and made me suffer.

My neighbours did not keep quiet either. They began to warn my mother, 'Hey, you Ceylonese woman! If you don't put a stop to this, your boy will run away to Bombay.' When I heard them, I wondered if I could turn into a woman if I went to Bombay.

The young men on the street began to call me '*ali*' and '*ombodu*'. They would say '*pottai*' to my face and laugh. I would tremble with humiliation. I would be tempted to throw stones at them for making fun of me. But how many people could I stone? My own brother and his friends would ridicule me.

5. The First Sacrifice

When I was six, there was a boy named Seelan who lived nearby. Our families had become good friends. Seelan was sixteen at the time. He enticed me to his house with the promise of playing some games. There, he asked me to commit sexual acts. I did everything that he asked me to do but it was not out of fear. At that point, I did not know what we were doing was wrong.

Seelan used me for his sexual needs whenever he had time. He would insert his penis between my thighs and penetrate me like he would a vagina. It would leave me out of breath. However, our relationship did not give me any happiness, just sorrow. There was only one reason for putting up with it—when no one understood me, he was the only person who thought of me as a woman and treated me as one. What he did with me is what a man does with women.

But Seelan's love, caresses and kisses were confined to the four walls of his room. He would often insult me in front of others and would pretend as if he was repulsed by my effeminacy. Seelan made me promise that I would not tell anyone about our relationship. Some years later, I learnt that Seelan had committed suicide.

As I spent most of my time with older people, I was rather precocious. Also, I had grown up watching television. Like the actresses on the screen, I wanted to be alone in a room with a man with whom I had a secret relationship. There, we would kiss and frolic.

From watching television, I had a rough idea of what married couples do in bed.

Watching Tamil movies made me long to get married. I asked Seelan to tie a *tali* around my neck. He immediately agreed and secretly tied the tali at the Ganesha temple on the banks of the river. I would hide the tali behind a picture of God at our home. When I was alone, I would put on a sari and tie the tali around my neck.

There was a bus driver who lived nearby. He must have been about thirty-five at the time. I was playing with my friends in front of his house when he called me inside. His wife and children were not at home. As we were talking, he took my hand and put it on his penis. I did not like what he did, and I certainly did not like him. I immediately screamed and called out to my friends as I ran out of that house. Why did he invite me in when there were so many other children around? Did he notice my effeminacy? After this incident, I stopped going there.

I would play in front of the temple near my house and eventually became friends with a man who visited the temple. He would lovingly embrace me and kiss my cheek. Even if it was ostensibly a kiss of affection, only I could feel the hidden desire behind the apparent affection. Even at that age, I could instantly identify men who had sexual intentions. However, he soon stopped coming to the temple. I would wait for him every day but he never came back.

Men evoked my desire from the time I was very young. Although I was a boy, I only desired men. I loved newly married men. I would try to seduce them with my femininity. If men I did not like approached or touched me, I would withdraw. I do not wish to hide the fact that even at that age I liked enslaving men with lust.

When I was eight, I had two friends at school. Their names were Ganesh and Vignesh. We would always sit together in class. During recess, we would share the lunches we brought from home. As we were talking, Ganesh told me that he was in a sexual relationship with his brother-in-law. Ganesh was effeminate too. We would be confused as we shared our experiences. Vignesh would listen to us talk. But he kept our secrets and would not tell anyone else.

I first learnt about transwomen on television. Later, I watched transwomen gather at the Kuthandavar temple in Koovagam, a temple where they had organised a festival for Aravan. 'Transwoman' was not a term that was used then. They would be called '*Aravani*'. When I saw the transwomen being married to Aravan, my heart was filled with joy. I longed to get married there. But at the time I did not think I belonged to the transwomen's community and did not want to live with them.

There was a time when I started losing hair and developed bald patches on my scalp. A neighbour said that I had an infection that led to hair loss and told me to apply *erukkam* milk to the bald patches. Instead of making my hair grow, the milk burnt my scalp. My classmates laughed at the sight of my head and called me 'baldy'. I was ashamed and shaved all my hair off.

That was when my sister's friend recommended a skin specialist. The specialist took a sample of my blood and told me that I was deficient in iron. He prescribed some pills and a medicinal oil to apply to my scalp. His treatment was successful. My hair grew back within a month.

I preferred to spend my time with animals rather than humans. I loved talking to animals. I think they understood what I said. Even today, animals grow fond of me at the very first meeting. In Kochadai, my friends were the goatherds, cowherds and most of the street dogs. However, Amma forbade me from befriending the cowherds. She was scared that they would kidnap me. I would get beaten all the more when I deliberately disobeyed her orders.

Violence at home would pursue me like a devil. I would be scared of the very people I was supposed to love. My sister would beat me, my brother would beat me, my mother would beat me and all the teachers in school would beat me. Beatings and insults were an inescapable part of my childhood. I still live with the fear of being beaten.

6. Beautiful Chennai

When I was nine, Appa sent us the legal documents for immigration. We moved to Chennai to take care of these official matters, as it would take a few months to complete all the formalities. We rented a house in a place called Kolathur, where my father's sister lived.

Although Chennai was a large city with tall apartment buildings, it lacked Madurai's natural beauty. There were no riverbanks and not as many trees and beautiful cows. More than anything, Chennai's drinking water didn't taste nice. I saw buffaloes for the first time in Chennai. I would caress the buffaloes and feed them grass. I also saw many baby tortoises during the monsoons. I would hold them and play with them.

I joined the sixth standard at the Danish Matric School, where I made several Muslim friends. One of them was named Nasar. However, I couldn't be close to the girls at the school as boys and girls were not allowed to mix with each other. I became friends with a couple of girls named Buvana and Nisha who lived in my neighbourhood.

The procedure for migrating to Germany grew complicated. Although we had sponsor letters from Appa that would reunite our family, the German embassy in India refused to give us a visa. We were asked to get our visas from the German embassy in Colombo.

However, as we had illegally entered India, it was not easy to return to Colombo. We would have to apply for a temporary passport at the Sri Lankan embassy and Shastri Bhavan in Chennai to atone for what we had done and get the Indian government's permission to emigrate.

Once we got permission, Amma left for Colombo leaving my sister and me with Mami, my father's sister. My brother also went to Colombo with my mother. To me, it did not feel like a major separation. If Amma was not around, she would not beat me. So, I was happy when she left.

But our aunt did not take proper care of my sister and me. Mami would eagerly take all the money my father sent her for our expenses. She would always be irritable if we spoke to her and would not even buy us the clothes that we needed. Mami would make an excuse that she was fasting to give us food that was inedible. If we asked her for new clothes, or fish or eggs with our meals, she would blatantly lie and say that she does not have any money. And when Appa would call, she would not let us talk to him properly.

I did so well at my new school that I was amazed at myself. As it was an English medium school, the school would punish us if we spoke in Tamil. When I secretly spoke in Tamil, all the other students would tease me for speaking with a Madurai accent. I became known as 'Madur' in school.

During vacations, I would fly kites and go cycling with my friends Nasar, Shridhar and Mahesh. Every Sunday I would visit the nearby church to participate in the service. Later, when I read the Bible, I was astonished to discover that it refers to transwomen as outcastes. In Chapter 56 of Isaiah, this is what Christ has to say about outcastes: 'Even unto them will I give in mine house and within my walls a place and a name better than that of sons and of daughters: I will give them an everlasting name that shall not be cut off.'

I would visit a temple on Fridays with my cousin Ramya and pray that she gets married soon. We would light lamps with sesame oil, and I would steal ghee from the lamps and eat it. Nasar would tell me a lot about the glories of Allah. I had unbounded love for Allah as well.

I learnt about the Islamic path from Nasar. I would visit his house and listen to his father's sermons. But what I liked most at Nasar's home was the sight of his brother. He must have been about twenty, I think. He looked majestic with his muscular body and flat stomach. I am deeply infatuated with firm-bodied men. Doesn't Lord Aravan have all the thirty-two signs of masculinity?

7. First Love

My cousin Mayuran lived with his parents and younger brother in a Chennai neighbourhood called Madipakkam. He was over twenty and very handsome. I would often visit his home, and he would frequent my place too. My attraction towards him soon grew into love. I liked the actors he liked. I would eat what he liked eating and I would even use the same perfume he used to remind me of his fragrance. We would cycle everywhere with me sitting in front of him on the crossbar of his bicycle looking like an overjoyed lover.

But I thought that it was one-sided, because Mayuran never gave me any importance. He never expressed his love for me. Instead, whenever he saw me, he would playfully hit me. I sometimes spent the night at his place. But if I entered his room, he would drive me away. I was not even ten years old then, but I would long for his love.

Mayuran's family had guests visiting one night when I was to stay there. So Mayuran asked me to sleep in his room. I thought my lover had finally acknowledged my love for him and almost jumped with joy. I ran into his room and lay next to him on the bed. I was unable to sleep because I was nervously wondering what would happen next. In a little while, I heard him snoring. He put his arm around me in his sleep. I forgot myself in the warmth of his body.

A little later, Mayuran whispered my name twice. I lay with my eyes closed and pretended that I had not heard anything. He thought I had fallen asleep and began to kiss me. I was amazed. Mayuran, who beat me in front of others, was kissing me! I still pretended to sleep. He took my hand and made me stroke his penis. He sucked my nipples. This boorish man's moustache pricked my body and gave me goosebumps. My heart was beating fast. But I continued pretending to be asleep. He soon came. A minute later I heard him snoring again.

The next morning, I was ashamed of myself. I asked myself whether I was responsible for provoking Mayuran. I hesitated to look at his face or talk to him that morning. That night, Mayuran asked me to sleep in his room again. With my heart yearning for love and my body longing for pleasure, I happily accepted his offer.

Mayuran immediately fell asleep because he was tired after a hectic day outside. Unable to control my desire, I spread my arms over him. I began to kiss his lips. I slowly reached for his penis. He suddenly woke up and grabbed my hand. I was astonished and fumbled because I did not know what to do.

'Thanujan! How do you know all this?' he asked me. I replied, 'When you did all those things to me yesterday, I was unable to sleep.' Mayuran responded, 'I knew you weren't asleep.' We did not waste time after that and devoted ourselves to the art of making love all night. Once he was done, he asked, 'Have you ever done this with anyone else?' One must not conceal the truth from one's lover, so I told him that I was in a relationship with Seelan. Mayuran laughed and said, 'You're so young yet so experienced!'

I learnt everything about sex from Mayuran. Once, he asked me to suck his penis. I was scared and refused. I was afraid of becoming pregnant. Mayuran said, 'If you truly love me, you'll do as I say.' When I understood that this was a way of proving my deep love for him, I did everything he asked me to do. I was madly in love with Mayuran. I wrote his name on the walls of my house and in my textbooks and spent most of my vacations at his house.

Then, Mayuran's uncle's daughters visited him. The elder sister was newly married. Her husband was in Canada and she would move there to be with him in a few days. The younger sister was very beautiful. Her name was Mohana and she must have been about eighteen. Both sisters liked me, and one evening, the three of us went to the neighboring Ganesh temple.

Mohana and I sat outside the temple and talked. She plucked a leaf from a plant and used its stem to write 'Mayuran' on the wall. My eyes were ablaze when I saw that. I wondered why she did what I liked to do. I pretended to tease her and asked, 'Mohana, do you like Mayuran?' She did not respond and gracefully plucked another leaf. She was bashful! I decided that I should not take it any further.

Then, with a serious expression on my face, I told her, 'Mayuran hits me. He's a drunk and smokes beedis and cigarettes. He's evil!' I gave her a list of complaints about Mayuran and tried to divert her attention to his brother by saying he was nicer. But she wasn't listening to me. 'What time will Mayuran be back?' she asked.

How could I tell Mohana that Mayuran and I were in a romantic relationship? As she was his uncle's daughter, there was a strong possibility that they would get married. I felt miserable. I cried when I was alone. I was unable to kill and bury my love for Mayuran.

The next day, I asked Mayuran to marry me. He laughed and said, 'Are you crazy?' I suppressed my welling tears and asked him, 'Don't you love me?' He replied, 'Two men can neither love each other nor get married.' I asked him if he loved Mohana. He said yes and stared into my eyes. I looked at him and wondered silently, *Didn't you think of me as a woman when we were together?*

After this incident, I stopped going to Mayuran's house. I did not feel like meeting him. Although I was heartbroken by this betrayal, instead of hating Mohana I grew fond of her. Why could I not have been her? Had I been her, I would have spent all my life with my lover, who was dearer to me than life itself!

I raised three stray dogs in Kolathur. I named them Blackie, Brownie and Whitie. I once cycled to a nearby shop to buy them something to eat. As I was talking to the shopkeeper, I heard loud clapping behind me. I turned in alarm. There were two transwomen who were clapping their hands and asking the shopkeeper for money.

I grew agitated when I saw them. I knew that it was people like them who attended the Koovagam festival to get married to Lord Aravan. They looked like men, but they were wearing saris. I saw people laughing and making fun of them. There were some young boys leading the crowd who jeered and teased them by calling them 'ombodu', 'pottai' and 'ussu'. But I thought I was looking at two angels.

They went begging to every shop. I followed them on my bicycle. They did not notice me because I was just a small boy. Wherever they went, there would be a commotion. After following them for a short while, I went back home. Although I admired them, I was scared that they would kidnap me and take me to Mumbai.

If I had continued to stay in India, I might have joined the transwomen, and my life would have taken a different turn. But my sister and I had to return to Sri Lanka.

8. Colombo

During this period, my mother went to Germany along with my brother. There were some legal complications that prevented me and my sister from going with them. There were certain compulsions that meant that my brother would have to be sent first. Our parents asked us to stay with some relatives in Colombo, where our living arrangements had been made with a cousin of Amma's. We called him Nesan Mama.

Mama lived in a place called Vellavathai in a large house along with his mother, his younger brother Vinu and their maid, Mathiakka. Mama's eldest sister, whom we called Bama Mami, also stayed with them along with her two children, Ajivan and Divya. The beach was a five-minute walk from their home. Mama's jewellery shop and groundnut store were on the Colombo–Kali road off the highway to Vellavathai. Those who worked at the store lived in small rooms behind the building, while Mama's house was on the top floor.

His house was like a wedding hall. Guests would always visit. People who worked in offices in Colombo or were going abroad would stay at Mama's place. My sister and I were intimidated by the crowds, the new faces and their ostentatiousness. We began our days in Colombo feeling shy and hesitant. Our circumstances drew us together. My sister became like a mother to me. She took great care of me.

I soon became close friends with Ajivan. He spoke Sinhala with ease as he had grown up in Colombo. Like me, he was known for being mischievous. We would fool old people, call them names, and run away. We also liked playing cricket on the beach and video games on Vinu Mama's computer. Divya too became a good friend. Unlike us, Divya and my sister could not step out of the house whenever they wished to—because they were girls. When I was at home, I would play with Divya. I would help Mathiakka cook by cutting vegetables.

Mama enrolled me in a German class. He did not want my sister to join the class because she had come of age. I was the only boy in the class. The rest were all newly married women whose husbands were in Germany. They were waiting for their visas from the German embassy in Colombo. I liked going to that class. Bama Mami made me join a computer class.

She had a bad habit of beating children. So, I would keep away from her.

Vinu Mama liked me. He would ask me to buy cigarettes for him. I would go to the closest shop, where the owner's son would sometimes be sitting at the counter. He was a university student for whom caressing my hand was more important than business. He would mumble loving words to me as if he were talking to a woman. I knew very well why he did that and would imagine what might happen if I ended up being alone with him.

I would often visit one of the people who worked at Mama's jewellery store. I would talk to him about cinema and jewellery. Once, he embraced me. He did not seem to fear the possibility of someone entering the room. Lust had dulled his mind. I pushed him aside and ran away. I never entered his room again.

I was sexually harassed a lot more in Sri Lanka than I was in India. When men discovered my effeminacy, they never feared touching me. They would make me sit on their laps and I would feel their penises swell under my buttocks. Even if I tried to avoid them, they would not let me go.

Vinu Mama did not talk much with me. But I would savour every word he said. He was twenty-five then. He had a proud swagger, and I was drawn to his majestic bearing. However, when he discovered my effeminacy, he began to beat me. He would beat me every day. The more he beat me, the more I was drawn to him. I think it was because of the influence of Tamil cinema.

One of the people who worked at Mama's jewellery store pierced children's ears. I eagerly asked him, 'Could you pierce my ears too?' The good-hearted man asked me to bring him some earrings. I could feel my desire grabbing me by the scruff of my neck and pulling me along as I ran at the speed of a bullet to my sister. I begged her to give me a pair of gold earrings, which she did. I ran back to the store, where the man pierced my ears in a second.

I could not think of anything but the earrings I was wearing. I did not think of the consequences. When I returned home wearing those earrings, one of my relatives looked at my ears and told my sister, 'Your brother has turned into a woman.' Bama Mami was shocked to see my ears and covered her mouth with her hands. However, my sister looked at me calmly. She had begun to understand me.

When Vinu Mama returned home and heard that I had pierced my ears, he was furious. He asked me to remove my earrings and kicked and pummelled me. I removed the earrings because I could not take the pain. Vinu Mama also scolded my sister for giving me the earrings.

A little later, my sister came and asked me to fill the piercings in my ears with small neem sticks to prevent them from closing. I did what she said. However, Ajivan told Vinu Mama what I had done. He thrashed me again. I bitterly got rid of the neem sticks.

I was prohibited from entering the kitchen and talking with the women to ensure that my effeminacy disappeared and my masculinity sprang forth. I would only remove my shirt when I was bathing. I was too embarrassed to be bare-bodied. Vinu Mama would forbid me from wearing a shirt inside the house. The entire family had taken an oath to turn me into a man. I was often thrashed.

I was repressed and isolated and was unable to bear the loneliness. I felt as if I had been set on fire. I created two imaginary female friends from that fire. I would tell them all my secrets, desires and wishes. These 'conversations' gave me some relief. I imagined my good thoughts were one of the friends and my evil thoughts the other. I would talk to these imaginary people even when I was walking on the street.

There was no sound of a crow cawing, heralding a guest, when Mayuran suddenly appeared at Mama's house. I saw him for the first time in six months. He narrowed his eyes and looked at me in wonder. 'Have you forgotten me?' I asked. My accursed love for him still tortured me. He said with indifference, 'Why should I remember you?' During lunch, Mama casually asked me, 'Do you know Mayuran?' I shook my head to say no as I swallowed my anger along with my food.

Someone in the neighbourhood was offering a course on cosmetics. Bama Mami enrolled my sister in the course. I was eager to take the course as well. But my wish remained unfulfilled because I was a man. I was very jealous of my sister. But as they say, something good can emerge from something unpleasant. My sister used me to try out everything that she learnt in the course. She threaded and corrected my eyebrows and made me wear saris in different ways. I liked helping her practise her new skills.

My immigration to Germany remained a problem because I did not have a birth certificate. I was only three months old when I first came to India, so I had not been registered anywhere. Without a birth certificate, I could not get a Sri Lankan passport. This delayed my move to Germany. My sister applied for a visa at the German consulate with the help of Appa's sponsor letter. But her application was rejected because she was already seventeen, and according to German immigration laws, those who are sixteen and older are considered adults. My mother returned to Sri Lanka to resolve these issues.

9. Amma's Arrival

It had been a year and a half since I had last seen my mother. My sister and I accompanied Nesan Mama to the Kattanayaka Airport to receive her when she arrived from Germany. We were filled with joy to see her. Amma brought many gifts with her. Germany had really transformed her appearance and disposition.

We stayed at a hotel in Vellavathai. There were facilities to cook there. We saw many other families and individuals there who were waiting to go abroad. In Colombo, there were more agencies for illegal emigrations than there were temples. They were more important than places of worship.

I met an assistant from one of those agencies. His name was Senthuran and he looked like he was in his twenties. Senthuran would visit the hotel every evening because one of the rooms there was full of people waiting to hear from his agency. They were all young men.

I would occasionally visit that room and try to befriend those young men, but they would only ask about my sister. However, I did not find anyone among them attractive. It was Senthuran who drew my attention. He wore stylish clothes and looked handsome. My heart was once again filled with love. I was just eleven then.

I wanted his love rather than his lust. I did not know if he would love me. But I would wait for him in the evenings. Within a few days, we grew close. Our relationship grew like a storm to the extent that I would sit on his lap and chat with him. If his face rubbed against my cheek as we were speaking, my young body would feel thrilled. My buttocks could feel his stiff penis. That secret sign below his waist gave me the hope that I could bring him under my control.

Senthuran and I grew so close that people in the hotel would ask me, 'Your lover still hasn't come?' Although they playfully said 'lover', I found the word deeply arousing and seductive. Thoughts of Senthuran kept me awake at night. Waiting for him had become my life.

During the day, young couples would come to the hotel, book a room for an hour and leave. Although it was illegal to let out rooms like this, the law was not followed at that hotel. I was like a fruit that had prematurely ripened and had no trouble imagining what happened in those rooms. Love and lust flowed everywhere. At the beach, couples would hide behind umbrellas intoxicated by their lust for each other. At the temple, Valli and Devayanai sat on Kandan's lap. I began to believe that it was not wrong to have a sexual relationship with people I love.

10. Sexual Violence

There was a fifty-year-old Sinhala man called Jamesayya who was tasked with renovating the hotel. I would talk to him as well. He spoke a little Tamil. I learnt a few Sinhala words from him. Within a few days, Jamesayya discovered my effeminacy. When he began to touch and caress me in a rough manner, I began to avoid him. I did not want to get close to anyone else because I was deeply in love with Senthuran. But Jamesayya pursued and harassed me. I was unable to tell anyone and felt miserable. I could only tell my imaginary friends.

One lazy afternoon, as I was walking around the verandah of the hotel, a strong hand grabbed my arm and dragged me into a room. As I tripped and fell, Jamesayya's leg slammed the door shut. I gasped and struggled, unable to move. Jamesayya removed his penis from his pants and rubbed it against my stomach as he sunk his teeth into my neck. I shut my mouth in fear.

If I yelled, Jamesayya would have said, 'I did it because this boy is effeminate.' Or he would have probably blamed me for soliciting him. That would have been an insult to my mother and sister. Once Jamesayya was done, he stood up and warned me, 'Don't tell anyone about this.' Then he drove me away. His semen stuck to my belly. His saliva was on my neck. My body smelt of him. I rushed to the bathroom and sat under the tap. I washed myself with tears and water.

When I got the opportunity to meet Senthuran alone that evening, I cried and told him what happened. I asked him not to tell anyone else nor make an issue of this. Senthuran consoled me and asked my mother for her permission to take me out. He drove me around Colombo and we ate at an expensive hotel.

After that, I would go out with him every day. My mother did not create a fuss because she had complete faith in him. We would eat at McDonald's, KFC and some Chinese restaurants and later sit on the beach at night and talk. I could no longer suppress my feelings and confessed them to Senthuran.

I was amazed that he understood my love. But he was reluctant to have a relationship because I was a young boy. I tried to get rid of his hesitation by telling him all about my sexual experiences and romantic failures. My efforts were somewhat successful. Senthuran accepted my love.

He parked his car on the side of the road, and I fully surrendered to him. It was the best remedy for all my longings and sorrows. Whenever I had sex, I was a boy who assumed a feminine role. But those were the only times that anyone was willing to accept me as a woman.

My relationship with Senthuran was very different from my earlier relationships. He did not merely like me for my body. He told me many stories. He listened to everything I had to say. He warned me, 'Don't be careless and just trust anyone.' He asked me to let him know if I was ever sexually assaulted.

Neither Seelan nor Mayuran was as loving and concerned about me. More importantly, Senthuran treated me with respect. When I had sex with him, I did not want to show him my penis. He did not wish to see it either. He never touched my penis. We would kiss each other even after he came. He made me sleep on his lap.

One day, he told me he was moving to Canada. I was shocked. I asked him to marry me and live with me in Germany. He just smiled and said nothing. I never got an answer. He soon left for Canada. I never met Senthuran again. But his memory remains fresh in my mind. He may read this book and get in touch with me on Facebook or Instagram.

Senthuran's departure broke me. I prayed to God that he should be arrested by some country on his way to Canada and be brought back to Sri Lanka. But God was always deaf to my requests. I concluded that God had brought me into this world to spend my entire life being miserable and sad. I summoned my imaginary friends and wept as I told them about Senthuran.

11. Yazhpanam

On 22 February 2002, the A9 highway to Yazhpanam was reopened following an agreement between the Sri Lankan government and the Liberation Tigers to put an end to the war. Amma and I decided to apply for my birth certificate at the Yazhpanam court as I could not get one in Colombo.

We took a small bus from Colombo and travelled all night. At dawn, our bus was stopped by the army at the border. There were hundreds of vehicles lined up. We heard that the road to Yazhpanam would open at six. Once the road opened, our bus moved to the army inspection centre, where it was stopped and inspected.

The army questioned us in Sinhala. As I was a boy, the female soldiers who inspected the women inspected me as well. I had heard of the atrocities committed by the Sri Lankan army and was anxious until we crossed the inspection booth. But the women who inspected me spoke to me with affection. 'Which class are you in, brother?' they asked me in Sinhala.

Soon after the bus left, it stopped at the inspection centre of the Liberation Tigers. That was the first time I saw the Tigers. I was amazed to see their women fighters standing there. I had never even dreamt that Tamil women could be so majestic. They looked like nothing mattered more to them than their responsibilities. There was not much talk. But they thoroughly inspected us and our belongings.

As I reached Yazhpanam, I saw houses that had been destroyed during the war. All around us were charred buildings, bullet-ridden walls and people who were tired of the war. Yazhpanam was under the control of the army. The city was full of army personnel who inspired fear. I involuntarily closed my eyes whenever I saw an army vehicle. The sound of the vehicles was loud enough to deafen us.

We stayed for the night at a relative's house. The next morning, we rented a car and went to Mankumban, the village where I was born. There were army booths all along the way. We drove across a causeway in the middle of the sea. The island welcomed me with a lush carpet of palm, coconut, plantain and screw-pine trees. There were so many birds—storks, pigeons, mynas and woodpeckers!

Amma had returned to the land of her birth after eleven years. Tears streamed down her face. The plot of land where our house once stood had turned into a forest full of palm trees where snakes and insects lived. There were just four bare walls remaining of the house in which we had lived. There were less than ten families left in the village. The others had been displaced.

Once Amma was done crying, we went to Velanai in search of Mama. Mama's house was like a ruined palace. There were many animals and trees there. I liked that house a lot. I was eager to play with the creatures there. I wanted to enter the ruined houses nearby and catch hold of bats.

Amma struggled for a month before she managed to get my birth certificate at the Yazhpanam court. She and I immediately returned to Colombo, where she again left my sister and me with Nesan Mama and returned to Germany. I received my passport within two weeks. Now, a newly dated sponsor letter from Appa was all that was needed.

There was a church close to Mama's house. I would occasionally pray there. Plays and dances were being organised to celebrate Christmas. The administration was looking for enthusiastic young men to participate in the festivities. The young men were not as enthusiastic about the dance as they were about the play. I told one of the organisers, 'I don't know how to dance like a man, but I can dress up like a woman and dance well.' They happily welcomed and encouraged me.

As I was a good dancer, I stopped practising and paid attention to my costume and makeup. On the day before the dance, I applied henna on my arms and legs and slept on the terrace because of the heat. Someone told Vinu Mama about this. I could hear him as he came up the stairs. He rushed towards me to kick me. I stumbled to my feet when he slapped me hard on my cheeks. I could not take the assault and ran to take refuge behind Bama Mami.

As I hid behind her, I told Vinu Mama, 'I put on the henna for the dance.' When he understood that I was going to dance as a woman, he was all the more furious. But after Bama Mami told him it was being organised by the church, he cooled down a bit. He reluctantly agreed to let me participate in the dance programme.

Christmas began with some cultural programmes on stage. I wore a pavadai, a hair extension and makeup. I had to patiently await my turn in a room but went outside as I desperately had to pee. Some young men began whistling and teasing me when they saw me. They were also participating in the cultural programme. Although they knew that I was the one who was dressed up like a woman, they did not hesitate to tease me. Some of them squeezed my fake breasts. Some pinched my waist. Some tried to kiss my lips. Although I was irritated, I was secretly happy. I took their mischief and harassment as an acknowledgement of my femininity.

I was happy that I looked beautiful in my dress; that I looked like a real woman. Feeling enthusiastic and elated, I danced well. Once I was done, the hall resounded with applause. I wished to hear that applause all my life.

When I received Appa's new sponsor letter, I went to the German embassy to apply for a visa. I got my visa within a month. But my sister's case was still complicated. She had to battle with the law. Nesan Mama took just three days to arrange my trip to Germany. I would fly alone from Colombo on 11 February 2003. Nesan Mama, Bama Mami and my sister came to the airport to see me off.

At the airport, I was lucky to meet Manjula, a Tamil woman who was travelling on the same flight. Mama entrusted me to her. She was my support during the flight. Ten hours later, the flight landed in Düsseldorf. I was full of dreams when I first set foot on German soil. Germany must have sunk a little, unable to bear the weight of my dreams.

12. Willkommen

Amma's younger sister Vasuki was waiting for me at the airport with her family. My brother was there too. Vasuki had two children. Her husband, Chithappa, seemed to have a gentle nature. It was a harsh winter. My aunt had brought me some winter clothes, but even after wearing those clothes, my palms were cold. The apartment where my family lived was in Aachen. It took us an hour to reach there.

Amma had cooked a feast and was waiting for us. Appa was at work when we arrived. He worked at a restaurant in a major hospital. A little later, Appa came home. He shook hands with me like a foreigner. He did not ask me how I was and instead chatted with Chithappa. He had not changed at all.

This became clearer as the days went by. Appa was never kind to us. He did not respect Amma either. If we went out as a family, we would run behind him like puppies. He would not tell us where he was going. He never bought me anything I wanted. He would not answer any of my eager questions. And even if he did, he would lie to evade them.

There were two bedrooms in our apartment in Germany. I was to sleep in my brother's room in a separate bed. At first, I did not know what to do with my time. I could not understand the shows on television. My only solace was playing games on my brother's computer when he was out. That was a time when I was addicted to computer games.

When Appa was not at home, I would dress up in my mother's clothes, tie a towel around my head like a wig and sing and dance to Tamil movie songs. Amma would not say anything as she had seen me sing and dance from the time I was little.

After a few days, my brother took me to a school. *'Willkommen'* was engraved at the entrance of this very large school. It meant 'welcome'. I joined a German language course that was open to new immigrants who were under eighteen. There were students from many countries, including Thailand, Pakistan, Afghanistan, Iraq, Russia, China, Ghana and Kenya. There was no other Tamil student. The senior students in our class spoke fluent German as they had joined the course some months earlier. Benny, an eleven-year-old student from Kenya, had joined the course a day before me. He and I struggled with German.

Some of the students began to beat and tease us because we were younger and smaller. We languished because we were scared and lost. Besides Benny, no other student tried to befriend me. No one was loving or supportive. The only good thing was that the teachers there never beat us.

During breaks, the students would engage in fights. I cautiously withdrew. The senior students would call me *'schwul'*. I did not know what it meant. When I asked my brother what it meant, he was irritated. He replied, 'That's what you are.'

The nickname spread like wildfire across the school. They called me schwul in my presence and behind my back. I later learnt that schwul was a vulgar word that referred to homosexuals. Schwul was like *'kambi'* and *'sappai'*, vulgar words used by Sri Lankans to refer to male and female homosexuals.

We had sports in school but I did not enjoy playing them. I had to change my clothes in front of the other boys. I felt what a woman who had to change her clothes in a room full of men would feel. When we played football, some of my fellow students would intentionally kick the ball at me. Despite all the beatings, abuses and teasing, I learnt to fluently speak and write German within six months. I was given permission to join the same school in the sixth grade after the summer vacation.

There were roughly forty Tamil families from Sri Lanka living in Aachen. If I saw Tamils on the road, I would not hesitate to speak to them in Tamil. They would say a few words and end the conversation. Everyone here was in a rush. I shrank in the cold and in loneliness as well. After all, I was a child who had once played in the scorching heat of Madurai and Chennai!

My brother installed our first internet connection. He relented and agreed to teach me how to use the internet when I begged him. The internet opened up a new world for me at a time when I was so lonely. I learnt many new things. I made many friends through the internet. I did not know then that the virtual world would upset my entire life. I searched for the meaning of the English word 'gay'. Many gay pornographic videos appeared on the screen. I discovered that it was not that rare for two men to have sex.

During the summer vacations, my aunt Vasuki would take us to her home. Visiting her house made me happy.

I liked playing with her children and Chithappa was not hard-hearted like Appa. Chithappa was very loving towards his children and would buy them anything they asked for. He loved his wife, too. But, more importantly for me, they always had many things to eat.

I would compare them to my family, where Appa would come home drunk every night and beat me and Amma. Unlike Chithappa, Appa neither had a car nor a driving license. His drinking and gambling had left him in debt.

I knew many things that I was not supposed to know from the time I was very young. But I only discovered caste for the first time after I moved to Germany. Whenever my relatives gathered, caste was an important topic of discussion. They were like flies floating in the sewage of their Vellala caste. My father knew the caste identities of the Tamil families that lived in Aachen like the back of his hand. The children in all our families were strictly forbidden from visiting the houses of those who were not Vellala and from eating their food. I violated this rule like I did all the other rules. My father beat me for it.

I joined the sixth grade after the summer vacation. There were fourteen female students and twelve male students in my class. My teacher, Clara, was very loving and concerned about me. She has helped me at various moments in my life. Although I was from a famous seaside village, I did not know how to swim. Clara arranged swimming lessons for me. I found that I could swim after only two sessions.

We learnt about the Liberation Tigers from the Tamil television programmes that were broadcast by the Eezham Tamil diaspora. They were all sympathetic towards the Tigers. When I noticed that I was surrounded by people who loved and supported the Liberation

Tigers, I too became a devotee. The inhumanities that were being meted out to the Sri Lankan Tamils made me think. I thought I should study well and become a doctor and go to Vanni to serve my people there. I wanted to learn my mother tongue.

I studied the Tamil language every Saturday at classes held at a school in our city. Although I had Tamil as a subject in the sixth grade in India, I could only join the second-grade students in that school. I soon made many friends in the Tamil class. There was a girl called Aparna who was my age. We became close friends.

This school had stricter rules than the school in India. The management was rife with corruption and family politics. Many of the diasporic Tamil organisations were marred by flaws and irregularities. From temples to schools, corruption was rampant.

13. World Wide Web

After I turned thirteen, my brother introduced me to a virtual chat room called tamilchatworld.com. When my brother was not at home, I would chat under the name 'Mohana'. I loved that name because Mayuran was in love with Mohana. When they saw that name, several men would chat with me. I told them I was eighteen. No one knew how anyone looked. I was happy and excited to chat with them. This is how I met Arun. He was in Germany too.

He asked me for my phone number. My brother had given me his old cell phone to use. I gave Arun the number on an impulse. He called me immediately. I hesitated to answer his calls, but he kept calling. Finally, I went to the balcony and spoke to him in a hushed voice. My body trembled in fear. We must have spoken for five minutes. Arun did not realise I was a boy because I had a feminine voice.

After a few phone conversations, he asked me for my address. I gave him a fake address. He began to threaten me as the days went by and pestered me to meet him. Eventually, I severed all ties with him. He became furious and shared my number with several Tamil men in the region. That the German telecommunication department did not collapse from the number of phone calls I received is a wonder!

No one who spoke to me over the phone realised that I was not a girl but a thirteen-year-old boy. From the countless sexual and abusive calls, I made a few good friends. Two of them, Pradeep and Sendil, were affectionate and respectful. Sendil even introduced me to his wife. I have had a lasting friendship with Sendil.

We were introduced to sexuality and reproduction in our science classes at school. Although we were introduced to homosexuals, bisexuals and heterosexuals, there was nothing on transwomen or transmen. I did not know anything about transwomen at that point. I assumed that men who were effeminate and had the courage to resist their families became women and those who did not were homosexuals. After some deep thought, I arrived at the conclusion that I was homosexual. I thought I had become one because of my childhood desire for men. I was endlessly anxious that I would not get married and have children. My anxiety led to irrepressible rage. I grew resentful of those who had used me for their sexual desires.

Soliciting someone who was not eighteen was a punishable offence in Germany. The punishment was severe. Anyone who touched your private parts without your consent would be imprisoned for a few years. The law is applicable even if it is your own father. Children in school are introduced to good and bad touch. There are elaborate discussions on sexual offences to create awareness. If such education had existed in schools in India, I could have avoided many terrible experiences.

As I deeply thought about all this, I thought of my past and began to feel sad. I decided that I must reform my life and live like a man. The first thing I did to act on my decision was to watch pornographic movies to evoke my desire for women. I thought that I would get aroused if I looked at their naked bodies. But nothing of the sort happened. Instead, I longed to be like the women in the movies.

I was conflicted and cried at the thought of not having bodies like theirs. But I did not give up. I tried to talk and walk like a man. But my irrepressible femininity did not let me sustain the pretence. A pregnancy can be concealed for a few months, but I could not conceal my femininity even for a day.

In Germany, I did not live the comfortable life that I had lived in India and Sri Lanka. Appa was the only earning member of the family. But he was debt-ridden. He would not even give me loose change for my expenses and did not take care of my basic needs. I could not go on school excursions because I did not have money. If I asked for anything, my father would slap me. Sometimes, even my brother would thrash me. His anger and resentment towards the family were directed towards me.

Appa did not care about my well-being. He did not know how old I was or which class I was in. I could never have gone to Germany if not for my mother's efforts. My family was crippled like a temple chariot that cannot move without an axle. What was astonishing is that our circle of relatives thought of my father as a gentleman. They extolled him for being a responsible family man. Appa behaved like a gentleman in front of others, but he revealed his true self at home.

There was not a day when he did not beat us. He was generous with his use of swear words. I learnt many swear words from him. When Appa turned violent, I would think of complaining to the police. But I tolerated the beatings because I was scared that if I reported the violence to the school or the police, the government would take me away and put me in a foster home.

My brother had a close friend named Babu, who ran a provision store with his wife in our city. They needed someone to take care of their baby boy. When I visited their house, Babu and his family noticed how happy I was playing with the child. They asked me if I could watch the child after school for 200 euros a month. I happily accepted their offer. They were happy too, because other babysitters would charge three times that amount.

I would rush to Babu's place every day after school. I took great care of the child. I was overjoyed when I was with the child. I lived like a mother those days, feeding and bathing the child. I thought that I would never have a child of my own, so I loved Babu's son as my own child. I put him on my lap and sang him to sleep. Once he was asleep, I would chat with men on the phone.

My sister did not get her German visa from the German consulate in Colombo. Amma was distressed at the thought of a young unmarried woman living alone at home. My uncle who was in Switzerland offered to help us. With the help of his travel agent, my sister managed to go to Switzerland. There, she applied for asylum.

Amma and I went to Switzerland to see her. My father was indifferent. He was always in a state of drunken revelry, gambling away his money on cards and beating me if there was nothing else to do.

14. Forest Dwellers and Hip Hop

The white students at my school ridiculed those who were dark-skinned by calling them 'forest dwellers' and 'black monkeys'. I was ridiculed even more for being an effeminate Eezham barbarian. I became infamous for my effeminacy in school. Because of the jokes and teasing, I would avoid male students standing in a group. I would tremble with fear at the thought of being beaten up.

I went to school every day feeling scared. All my friends in school were girls. I joined the girls' hip-hop group and learnt to dance. I would dance with my female friends during the school's festivals. I was the only boy at school who danced. Dancing always gave me joy and relief. My inborn talent persists today in the era of TikTok.

My female friends gradually grew protective of me. If anyone tried to insult me, they would drive them away. Although their support was somewhat comforting, I had to confront another problem. I could not stand before the other students and talk. When teachers asked me questions, I was unable to clearly answer them. I was scared that someone would suddenly call me schwul. The teachers could not understand my problem, which affected my grades.

There was an insolent Turkish boy in my class named Ibrahim. His chief pastime was to beat and bully weaker students. I was a quiet, shy and effeminate student so my teacher asked Ibrahim, who was my complete opposite, to sit next to me. She thought Ibrahim would quieten down if he sat next to me.

The rude Ibrahim who asserted his authority by beating everyone up was only a little affectionate towards me. I helped him with his studies. I would teach him English. He would not bring any pens or books to school. I would lend him my books and pens.

Ibrahim became my guardian angel. He would ask me to join his group of friends. No one could touch me without his permission. I assumed his concern emerged from his love for me. Without giving it any further thought, I began to love Ibrahim because I was longing for love.

But there were two other people who were in love with me. They were both girls my age. Although I felt like a woman from within, I was a tall and handsome young man. Aparna from Tamil class was in love with me. I tried to love her back with the hope that I would become a man. But I was not attracted to her. I was waiting for the right moment to tell her that I felt like a woman.

One of the administrators at the school noticed that we were close and reproved me for being friendly with her. As far as he was concerned, it was wrong for a young man like me to be close to a woman. I was furious and stopped going to Tamil class. But the administrator complained to my parents. Although they knew I was effeminate, they warned me not to fall in love with Aparna because she belonged to a lower caste.

The other girl was a young Turkish woman who had followed me to my house with her friends. She had the courage to ask me for my number. I gave it to her. I had a wishful fantasy that this Turkish woman would reinforce my masculinity. I would chat with her over the phone. Once, we met at a park. Although we walked around for an hour, I felt no love for her. My mind was filled with thoughts of the rude Ibrahim.

There was an Albanian beauty in our school named Kim who sparkled like a star. I was heartbroken when I discovered that Ibrahim was in love with her. I saw him kiss her on the lips during lunch break. I was unable to bear the pain and disappointment. My body grew cold and I trembled. I told Clara, my class teacher, that my chest hurt and then I went home.

Clara called me that evening and anxiously asked me how I felt. I was miserable and did not know with whom to share my sorrow. I gave in to Clara's affection and said, 'I'm in love with Ibrahim.' When she heard that, she cried, 'Oh *mein gott*!' Then she gave me some advice. 'See, Thanujan,' she said, 'Ibrahim will never love you back. Don't tell anyone at school about this because it will create unnecessary problems!' Like Clara who cried out to God, I cried out to my imaginary friends and unburdened my heart.

I looked for other friends to assuage my disappointment with Ibrahim. There was a section on Yahoo Messenger where one could chat with homosexuals. There were homosexuals from several countries there. I looked for friends there. But they were only interested in virtually satisfying their sexual desires. Those who were on the Tamil chat website where I was a member only wanted to be desired. The love and compassion that I was looking for was out of reach.

I could not find answers to questions that concerned my gender identity. My deep loneliness and the thought that no one understood me made me feel terribly depressed. I began to hate Ibrahim. I hated my family too. The only thing that I felt was hatred. There was a pervasive feeling of self-hatred as well. I would wet my pillow with tears every night thinking of my effeminacy that was responsible for all my sorrows. During the day, I walked about like a living corpse.

Once I was waiting for the bus after babysitting Babu's child. It was around 10 p.m. An old white man standing nearby beckoned to me. When I asked him what he wanted, he said, 'I have fifty euros. Will you have sex with me?' I withdrew in fear and ran away. I kept looking back to see if he was chasing me.

When I reached home, I told Amma about this. I did not tell her that he had asked me to have sex with him, but I anxiously told her that he tried to kidnap me. My mother was unconcerned. 'What would he do if he kidnapped you?' she asked. I felt an overwhelming sense of anger and hatred towards her. It was because of her indifference that I was sexually assaulted at an age when I could barely speak. How could I explain this to her?

A cousin from Madurai had moved to Paris. When I called him, I learnt that Mayuran was in Paris too. My heart began to race when I heard his name. I was eager to see him. I went to Paris the following Saturday. When I went to my cousin's place, he sized me up and said, 'You're still effeminate? When are you going to change?' I did not reply. Was I here to answer his questions? I wanted to talk to Mayuran and asked for his number.

Mayuran was shocked when he heard my voice. He asked me to come over to his house. My heart raced with joy until I arrived there and discovered that he had married Mohana a month ago in a civil union. She was soon going to join him in Paris. Mayuran showed me the wedding video on his phone. I was furious when I saw it. 'Why are you showing me this?' I hissed. But I managed to calm myself and said, 'Mayuran, I have travelled a long distance to meet you because I like you a lot. But you're telling me about your wedding and your wife.' Mayuran interrupted me and said, 'You still haven't changed? Don't be a fool. If you continue to behave like a woman, no one will respect you.'

He began to give me a lot of unnecessary advice. I was tempted to ask him why he did not think about all this when he used me in bed. I silently listened to him because sorrow had made me tongue-tied. Somewhere in the corner of my heart, I still loved him. Mayuran asked me to eat something before leaving. But my heart cried and I wanted to leave that very instant.

I left with that love in my heart. On my way back to Germany, a million questions pierced my heart like needles. Was what I felt for Mayuran love? I was not sure if I was deceiving myself. Such stories do not exist even in movies or on television.

Did Mayuran never love me? Did he merely use me for his sexual pleasure? Was my body responsible for my sorrows and humiliations? Did my feelings not matter at all?

15. Thirty Pills

I began to suffer from severe depression because I did not have anyone to share my problems with. My brother would beat me every day and ask me to behave like a man. My mother did not understand me at all. My father was hostile and rejected me. There was no room for my desires and wishes in my house.

Guests who visited our home ridiculed me for being effeminate. They would insult me by comparing me to my brother. My classmates at school teased me and the lover that I had eagerly gone in search of had insulted me. I decided that the only permanent solution to all of this would be to leave this world.

I took thirty paracetamol pills at midnight and lay down. I got up at five with a splitting headache. Terrified, I shook my mother who was sleeping and muttered, 'I have a severe headache.' She replied, 'Take a painkiller and go to sleep.' I told her that my head ached because I took thirty of them.

Amma was alarmed and woke my brother up. 'Why did you do this?' they asked as I silently held my head. Appa woke up to the commotion and asked the others what happened before going back to sleep. An ambulance was called and it took me to the hospital. They dissolved coal in water and poured it into my mouth to make me vomit. I nearly vomited my insides out and fell asleep exhausted.

The day after, a psychologist came to talk to me. He asked me why I had tried to kill myself. I replied, 'I scored low in the school exams.' That was what Amma had strictly asked me to say at the hospital. Then, I was visited by a nun who would occasionally visit the hospital to speak to the patients. She said, 'Committing suicide is a sin.' I opened my heart to her and said, 'I am not attracted to women. I'm only attracted to men.' She said that I had been possessed by Satan.

The doctors, the experts, the renunciants—not one of them understood my problem. My family concealed my suicide attempt from my relatives and neighbours out of shame. But I could not conceal my femininity even if I wanted to. Even God could not. No, not even Satan!

16. A Search for My Own Gender Identity

I wished to live like a woman. It was destined by nature. My body did not cooperate with my heart as it was subject to nature's law. I became anxious when I started to grow facial hair. I was disgusted as though my face had been infected. I shaved my face and then all my body hair and wore makeup to conceal my emerging beard. I applied clear coat nail polish on my nails and used women's perfumes. I would never step out without doing all this. This is how I went to school. I was particular about my feminine appearance precisely because I hated being teased and ridiculed for being effeminate.

Babu offered me a part-time job at his provision store. I would work at Babu's shop after school and return home at 8 p.m. I had to work on weekends too. My salary was 500 euros a month, but I would give half of it to my mother. It somewhat relieved my family's financial crisis.

For someone feminine like me, it was a challenge to work in that store. The store was frequented by drunks and vagabonds because it sold cigarettes and alcohol. Some of the men who noticed my effeminacy would write down their phone number and give it to me before leaving. Some womanisers would scratch my palm under the pretext of shaking hands. It was a sign that meant 'I want to have sex with you'.

There was a computer at the shop that had an internet connection. I would spend time browsing the internet when there were no customers. Looking for answers to the questions in my heart, I watched documentaries and videos on queer people and transwomen. Most of the documentaries on transwomen were made in Asia or the USA. I did not find any information on transwomen living in Germany.

I found some videos on Indian transwomen. In one of these videos, there was a Tamil transwoman named Angel who described the lives and struggles of transwomen in India. Then, I watched a Singapore Tamil television programme about transwomen. A transwoman named Buvana spoke about her life and the challenges she had to face.

Buvana was very beautiful. She spoke fluent Tamil and English. Her voice was just like a woman's. Buvana was emphatic when she said that transwomen suffer because of their lives as sex workers and that they should leave their jobs. When she described her childhood and her journey, it resembled my own life. I would cry every day watching her videos.

Through Buvana's videos, I discovered that anyone could acquire a feminine body with hormonal pills and that one could get gender reassignment surgery done in Thailand. Her words made a bright ladder descend into my prison-like heart that was enveloped in darkness. I was filled with determination to break through all obstacles like Buvana and live like a complete woman.

I also listened to an interview with Sukanya, a Malaysian transwoman. She was interviewed along with her mother. She looked like a beautiful angel with long hair that touched her waist. Sukanya lived with her mother in a large house and they ran a restaurant together. She also did social work. Seeing her life, I was gradually filled with hope and had a grip on the future.

In 2007, a website reported that someone from Kerala had become Mr Gay Europe. He lived in Hamburg in northern Germany. I thought I should contact him. After a tireless search, I found his email address and emailed him with some questions. I asked him, 'Why wouldn't a gay person like you become a transwoman?' He replied, 'I like being a man.' I did not understand his response. But our friendship lasted. I never stopped asking all the queer people I met then why they had not become transwomen.

I once watched a television show on the internet called *Ippadikku Rose*. The anchor was a beautiful woman whose voice revealed her identity as a transwoman. I searched for anything that I could find on her. She had completed her higher education in the USA but was living in Chennai. I sent her an email to introduce myself and ask if I could talk to her. She wrote back to me that very day with her telephone number.

I was unable to suppress my excitement and gave her a call. I quickly told her my entire story. Talking to Rose made me feel ecstatic. It was as if I was talking to God. Rose patiently listened to what I had to say and, like a specialist in the field, spelt out the contradictions that constitute different genders.

She very patiently said that I was ignorant to think that my wish to become a woman was because of my disappointing sexual relationships. She even said that I was born with a woman's sensibility and that I was not a homosexual but a woman. She suggested that I complete my education and become a woman. I thought I had finally met my mentor.

I often called her and she slowly dispelled the veils of confusion that had shrouded my heart. I seriously began to think of all the ways I had of becoming a woman. I studied German medical practices that concerned gender reassignment surgeries and their laws on various websites and thought that these laws could not possibly have been formulated by a transwoman.

If someone who was born a man wanted to become a woman, they would have to consult a psychologist for at least two years. They would have to wear women's clothes for at least a year. Only then would the psychologist send the person to a doctor who would prescribe hormonal pills and do the gender reassignment surgery. These expenses would be covered by medical insurance. Only after that could one obtain legal documents certifying them to be a woman.

I shared my concerns with my class teacher. 'I believe I'm a woman,' I told Clara. 'I'm not a homosexual as you think. Can you accept me as a woman?' With tears in her eyes she embraced me and asked, 'What will you do now?' I said that I didn't know who could help me. Clara recommended a psychologist from Aachen and suggested that I visit him.

I called the psychologist for an appointment. But from our very first meeting, I knew that he knew nothing about transwomen. I still met him for an hour every week. He could not help me, but he listened to my stories without scowling. It was a relief to have someone patiently listen to me.

I became good friends not just with Rose but also with Angel. I frequently spoke to them on the phone. Through our conversations I learnt of the travails of Indian transwomen. A modern gender reassignment surgery was a fruit that was still out of their reach.

In those days, there were two ways in which Indian transwomen could transition. There was a ritual called *nirvanam* that was performed to get rid of the penis. The first way of severing the penis was called *tayamma kai*. The transwoman would give offerings to their goddess, Santhoshi Mata, along with the other transwomen before their penis and testicles were severed with a razor before a picture of the goddess. The one who severed the penis was known as a *tayamma* in the transwomen community. When Rose told me about this, my body shivered. I could not understand how they could sever the genitalia without any medical assistance.

The second way was for a doctor to remove the penis and testicles after putting the transwoman under anaesthesia. Whichever method was used to remove the genitalia, an orifice was left through which the transwoman could urinate. However, they could no longer have sex with a woman.

Rose told me that she was going to undergo a modern gender reassignment surgery in Thailand. I longed for the day when I would have the same surgery. I was confronted by a sense of emptiness. My male genitalia was an unwanted thing that hung from my body like a heavy burden.

Time was indifferent to my sorrow as it flew past. I scored the highest marks in my annual exams in 2007 and was given an award for being the best student at school. The news was even published in the local newspapers and some of the customers who visited Babu's store congratulated me.

But it made no impression on my family. While others celebrated my success, my father continued to thrash me. My brother always ridiculed me and called me names and my mother remained indifferent. My sister was far away. My family made no attempt to understand me.

Instead, they harassed me by insisting that I behave like a man. They wanted me to cut my hair short and not wear makeup. The more they did this, the stronger became my desire to live like a woman. I would go shopping with my female friends from school and buy dresses. Later, I'd secretly hide them in my cupboard. When I was in the bathroom, I would dress up like a woman.

17. The Magical Device

My sister gifted me a laptop for my birthday. Until then, I had been using my brother's computer when he was not at home. When I received my own laptop, I felt as if I had grown wings. I used my new laptop to meet many men on the internet. I chatted with them pretending to be a woman. The intonations of my voice when I spoke were more elegant than that of a cis woman because I longed to live like a woman.

That was how I met Kamal, who was a university student living in London. He would appear on webcam and wanted to see me as well. I would lie and tell him that I didn't have one. Kamal loved Tamil film songs, so I would sing to him every night. He would seduce me on camera.

It brought peace to my mind because he thought that I was a woman. I wore a dress and dared to show him my face on camera. I refused to show him anything below my neck. He still did not doubt that I was a woman. But a few days later, I no longer wished to keep the truth from him. 'I'm not a woman as you think I am,' I told him. 'I'm a transwoman who is waiting to become a woman.' Although he was a little shocked, he continued to have sexual conversations with me. I virtually satisfied his sexual desires.

I was chatting with a friend on the same website who introduced me to a Tamil radio show that was being broadcast in Canada. I took part in the show by calling in and speaking to the host. I was introduced as Mohana. I soon gained many fans because of my voice and the way I spoke. I chatted with them on the show's website. They spent their time chatting with me assuming that I was a woman. Many of these chats turned into intimate conversations over Skype. Everyone who chatted with me said that he was in love with me.

I explored all my options to become a woman. I thought the first step would be to make my family understand. I wrote a long email to my brother. I disclosed all my feelings and desires in that email. I said that I had been sexually assaulted and that my family had treated me worse than an animal. I ended the email by saying, 'If you don't like me, I'll live on my own. But no one can stop me from becoming a woman. I can't even stop myself.'

I received a brief response from my brother within a few hours. He wrote: 'You have to renounce your effeminacy for the sake of the family's honour.' I wrote back to my brother saying, 'Anna, please don't look for our family's honour in what is between my thighs.'

I thought I must tell Amma before she finds out from my brother. I summoned my courage and entered the kitchen. 'Amma, I need to speak to you,' I said. I came straight to the point and asked, 'Amma, can't you accept me as your daughter?'

Everything fell into place for Amma with that question. She had noticed me from the time I was a child. She was familiar with the differences in my body. I was born with a small penis. It was much smaller than the average penis of other boys my age.

But all this did not concern Amma. Her sole concern was the family's reputation. She threw the ladle in her hand at my face and began to yell, 'Is this why you grew your hair and pierced your ears?' She created a commotion and suggested that I go far away somewhere and end my own life. But I was determined and told my mother, 'I've decided to become a woman, not die.'

My sister called me from Switzerland the next day when I was working at the store. Amma had complained to her that her brother was going to turn into a woman. Unlike my mother and brother, my sister did not fight with me. She patiently listened to what I had to say and accepted my wish. 'Don't worry,' she said. 'I will talk to Amma and convince her. We live in Europe. We don't need to fear anyone.' When she said this, I was filled with joy and courage. As promised, she pacified Amma. I stopped talking to my brother. As for my father, I did not care. I disregarded him just like how he disregarded me.

One night, Amma spoke to me candidly. 'Thanujan, you shouldn't wish to become a woman,' she said. 'Dress up in women's clothes at home. But don't step out wearing them and ruin our reputation.' She begged me to promise her that I would not become a woman. 'I'm already a woman at heart,' I responded. Amma wiped her eyes and said, 'I know. When we were in Madurai, an astrologer told me you would turn into a woman.' That astrologer must have gauged my effeminacy from my demeanour.

18. A New School

I had scored well in my tenth-grade exams and joined a reputed school. It was called a gymnasium. I planned to study there for the next three years before joining a medical college. Gradually, I made female friends at the new school. I told them that I was waiting to become a woman. They were all happy when they heard that and wholeheartedly accepted me as one of them.

But my male classmates erected an imaginary wall between us. They did not talk to me. The news that I was going to become a woman quickly spread. I was on everyone's mind. I had to change clothes in the men's room during the sports break. Neither my classmates nor I liked it. They looked at me as if I was a strange creature.

This reputed school was a place where the greatest egotists studied. No one could surpass their racism, their gossip and their insults. A Kurdish student they had humiliated even died by suicide. I did not kill myself nor run away from that school because of two people—Ilene and Sara. They were my friends who protected me like a shield.

The curriculum in the new school was very rigorous. I stopped working for Babu because I had to spend all my time studying. Although I visited my psychologist from time to time, there was no progress. I kept asking my psychologist to get a doctor to prescribe hormone supplements, but I would have to wear women's clothes for at least a year before I could be prescribed hormones.

However, I hesitated to go to school or anywhere else in women's clothes because I had gained the muscular body of a young man and had begun to grow full facial hair. I feared that if someone who looked like a man dressed in female clothes, he could be beaten or even killed. My fear was justified as this was known to happen in Europe.

I only wore women's clothes when I visited my psychologist. But I lied to him that I always wore such clothes. As I mentioned, he did not know anything about transwomen. He became the primary reason for my distress when he was supposed to be treating me. He was determined to use me to extract money from the medical insurance company.

I lost faith in him and reduced the frequency of our meetings. When I met him for the last time, he fought with me and said that I was not coming to meet him on the days we had planned. He used some rude words to scold me. I ran out of his office and into the street with tears of rage. I thought I would throw some soil at that awful psychologist and curse him but there was not even a fistful of soil on the wretched streets of Aachen.

I was unable to concentrate on my studies as I grew increasingly stressed each day. I went to school only once or twice a week. No one spoke to me at home. I was unable to sleep at night and had tears in my eyes as I kept tossing and turning. And on the rare occasions when I slept, I would have nightmares and wake up screaming. Even my imaginary friends did not speak to me.

Who could I talk to? How could I sleep? I was anguished. I visited our family doctor and asked him to give me sleeping pills. He said sleeping pills are bad for the body and instead recommended a herbal potion that induces sleep. The potion helped me sleep a bit.

My classmate Sara—who was Turkish—introduced me to her cousin Bilquis, a plump twenty-four-year-old who lived alone. Bilquis treated me like a woman when she heard that I wanted to become one. This made me adore her. However, Bilquis had some psychological issues. At the hospital where she was being treated, a transwoman named Turna worked at the snack bar. Bilquis suggested that I meet Turna, as she could give me some sensible suggestions that might address my gender issues.

We met Turna the next day. She must have been about forty and looked like a man dressed in female clothes. We talked over a cup of coffee at the snack bar.

Turna said that a good psychologist's service and help are necessary if one wants to become a woman. She gave me the number of a psychologist in the city and said that she was confident that if I consulted this psychologist, I would transition in just two weeks.

I hesitatingly asked Turna, 'Why haven't you transitioned yet?' Turna gave me a sad smile and said, 'I still don't know who I am.' But I was sure I knew who I was. I was a woman without a doubt!

I called the psychologist Turna had recommended. She gave me an appointment for the following week. My hair had grown to my shoulders at the time and the psychologist was amazed when she saw me. 'Are you taking hormones?' she asked. I told her I wasn't. She smiled and said, 'You look just like a woman. Even your voice is like a woman's.' Her smile illuminated my heart with a ray of hope.

I could not control my joy when the counsellor said, 'Visit me next month. I will write you a prescription for hormone pills.' It was December at the time, so I had to wait until January. On the night of New Year's Eve, the streets, restaurants and discos were full of people. Everyone must have wished each other a Happy New Year with excitement. But I was alone at home looking at the street from my window. I did not know then that I would celebrate future New Year's Eves in different countries. My life was waiting to be turned upside down.

19. Kirsten and Murat

Kirsten was a student in my class. He would go out of his way to talk to me. Our friendship grew stronger when I learnt that he was gay. He often asked me to accompany him to a disco in Cologne, a nearby city.

I had never been to a disco, so I was reluctant to accept his invitation. But I soon had a growing desire to go.

I finally summoned my courage and accompanied Kirsten to Cologne one Saturday evening. Although I had been to that city many times, I did not know that it was a gay man's paradise. Kirsten asked me to dress like a man as the disco we were going to was largely frequented by gay men. I wore a beautiful white shirt and a pair of black trousers.

As we approached the disco, I saw large groups of gay men standing outside on the street. When I entered the disco, I witnessed a new world. There were more than a hundred gay men inside. They stood in pairs, embracing and kissing each other. Some gently caressed each other. I was a little astonished to see such openly amorous overtures.

Bright lights hurt my eyes. Lively music was playing. Kirsten was looking for someone specific, but no one approached me. I remained alone until it was time to go back home. I thought that it was probably because of my effeminacy and my long hair.

Kirsten introduced me to a website where I could make LGBT friends. I registered myself as a transwoman. That very day, I received emails from several men. I was astonished and happy to know that there were many men who wanted to get to know me and have a relationship with me even after learning that I was a transwoman.

I met Murat through that website. He was a thirty-year-old Turkish man. I was drawn to his videos on the site and we soon grew close. Though I was reluctant to meet him, I eventually agreed. We arranged to meet one Friday evening. I wore women's clothes and waited at a spot a short walk from my house. Murat arrived in his car and picked me up.

The sun soon set and darkness began to envelop us. Murat did not take me to a restaurant or a bar. He parked his car in a dark and isolated place. I noticed that he was tall and handsome. We sat in the car and talked for a while. Once we had overcome our initial awkwardness, he kissed me on my lips. There was something unusual about his touch. It was not the violent touch that I had encountered as a child. Murat's desire gave me goosebumps. His touch brought to life the woman in me.

We had sex. I did not remove my lower garments. He did not insist on it either. Once we were done, we were in each other's arms as we talked. I was overjoyed as I lay in the arms of a man in female clothes. I began reciting poems. He dropped me in front of my house before dawn the following morning.

We met every Saturday. He parked the car in the dark and we did the same things every time. However, I soon realised that Murat only wanted me for my body. I would have to suck his penis for more than twenty minutes. Murat would have had to pay at least fifty euros for a sex worker to do that. But he did not have to pay me anything. What we did in the car in the darkness left me confused.

The relationship came to an end after I found his Facebook profile. There, he had a picture of himself with his white girlfriend. I realised that he was already in a serious relationship and was just using me as a sex toy. I broke off all ties with him.

After that, I stayed trapped at home. I was suffocated by my loneliness, which enveloped me like smoke. I began to sleep during the day because I could not sleep at night. My desire to become a woman was what kept my soul from being destroyed. The internet was the only window between me and the world.

20. The Thief's Lover

I met Ramesh from Paris on the internet. I was seventeen then, and he was twenty-four. I was wearing makeup and dressed in female clothes when I spoke to him on a video chat. He assumed that I was a woman. Ramesh was very handsome and spoke fluent English with an American accent. He briefly told me about his own life and admitted to being a member of an infamous group of Tamil thugs in Paris.

Ramesh had been deported from Canada for his criminal activities and sent back to Sri Lanka. After that he migrated to France, where he remained unemployed. He was soon involved in several fights and became an expert in blackmailing people for money. I truly was drawn to thugs. This must also have been a consequence of watching Tamil cinema.

My heart began to race when I read on a website that a group of thugs had axed a young man on a Paris street known to have many Tamil-owned shops. When I tried to call Ramesh, I could not get through. I silently lamented the loss of that young man and hoped that it was not Ramesh.

Ramesh called me that night. He told me that the man who had died was his friend. 'They'll come for me next,' he claimed. 'If I die, will you attend my funeral?' I consoled him by replying, 'You'll live a long life, get married and have children.' He asked me, 'Who'd be willing to live with someone like me? Would you?' he asked. I replied, 'I'll answer your question tomorrow.'

I thought of Ramesh all night. I believed that it was a sign of love. When I spoke to him the next day, I told him that I was in love with him and wanted to live with him. Ramesh cried with joy when he heard this. He kept saying, 'Really?'

We spoke every day over the phone after that and our love for each other grew. I ecstatically told my sister and Bilquis about my new love. Bilquis was happy to hear it. My sister too said that she was happy but warned me to be careful.

I thought hard and fought with myself before finally deciding to tell Ramesh the truth. I called him and hesitatingly said, 'I am a transwoman.' He did not react with shock as I had feared he would. Instead, he asked me, 'Did you get your surgery done?' I lied because I was scared that he would abandon me if he knew the truth and said, 'Yes, a year ago.'

Ramesh casually revealed that he had met some transwomen and had had sex with them while he was in Malaysia waiting to go to Paris. He told me that he loved watching 'shemales' in pornographic movies. I was relieved to know that he knew something about transwomen. He even said that he would often go to Zurich to visit his friends and had learnt that there were Malaysian transwomen working as sex workers in that city. Ramesh told me that one of his friends was living with one such transwoman named Priya and was particular to mention that he had lent her a lot of money. I soon understood what he meant.

Some days later, Ramesh told me he was steeped in debt and asked me for money. 'Imagine that you're helping your husband,' he pleaded. I was moved by his plea and sent him a share of the little money that I had saved. It was a big mistake. He began to demand more money at frequent intervals. If I said no, he abused me.

Soon, I had given him all my savings, tearfully imploring him to love me. I struggled to sustain this relationship when Ramesh asked me to come to Paris. His invitation got me excited. Even if he abused me, he was still my lover, wasn't he? I was desperate to meet him. I told only Bilquis that I was going to meet him.

I had never worn women's clothes outside of Aachen. My body trembled at the thought of travelling to Paris in women's clothes. I would have to put up with amused expressions and ridicule. Somebody could even attack me on the train. There were several young neo-Nazis around who hated transwomen and foreigners. The other problem was that I had fast-growing facial hair. I did not know how I could conceal it from Ramesh over the next two days.

It was on a Friday in January 2009 that I made my trip to Paris. I went to Bilquis' room early that morning. She lined my eyes with kohl, applied some fine makeup to my face and fixed an extension to my hair. I gave her a hug to thank her before rushing to the railway station.

The train from Aachen to Paris left at 8 a.m. The trip would take three hours. I was unsettled by hundreds of fantasies and thousands of dilemmas. Ramesh would be waiting for me at the Paris railway station. Throughout the journey, I thought what his reaction would be when he saw me.

Ramesh was waiting at the railway station as I had expected. I hesitated to approach him. I called him on his phone and said, 'I'm standing behind you.' He turned around and looked at me. I did not see any emotion on his face. He gestured for me to follow him. He briskly walked ahead of me as I tried to keep up, feeling a little shy and hesitant.

We soon arrived at a hotel. He asked me for a hundred euros to pay for the room. I did not have a lot of money, so I hesitated. 'I'll pay you back tomorrow,' he said as he snatched the money from my hand. He did not try to say anything else or even touch me until we reached the room. But once we were inside, he hugged and kissed me.

'Are you seeing me only now?' I asked, but he brushed off my question by saying, 'Let's not waste time talking.' He made me lean against the wall and kissed me. I loved him so much that I dissolved into a flurry of kisses. He removed his clothes and tried to remove mine as well. I asked him not to remove my trousers. He narrowed his eyes and looked at me. 'After we get married,' I said, 'I'll get my penis replaced with a surgically implanted vagina.' He did not insist further.

Before I left my house, I tucked my penis between my thighs and wore tight underwear. Even if someone felt my thighs, they would not find my penis. When Ramesh tried to remove my brassiere, I felt ashamed and said, 'There's nothing there.' I had never taken hormone pills, my breasts had not grown. He did not care and sucked my nipples. I was immersed in joy.

I sucked his penis. I did not hesitate to do it because my lack of a vagina and breasts made me feel inferior to women and sexual acts were the only means I had of retaining a man. He asked me if he could penetrate my anus. I refused. After he came, he lay on his back. I rested my head on his chest.

We made out several times that day. Although Ramesh wanted to have sex with me, there was no love or affection. He stepped out twice to get some food. If I had been a woman, we could have held hands and walked through the beautiful streets of Paris. He would have proudly introduced me to his friends. But I consoled myself with the thought that I was at least being treated like a woman in private.

We got up late the next morning. We took turns to bathe. When I stood before the mirror to do my makeup, he was standing close by. I noticed for the first time that he was shorter than me. I was five feet eleven inches tall. Most Tamil men were shorter than me.

Ramesh said that he was going to Switzerland with his friends that night. I was eager to go back home because I could not bear any further disappointment, so I asked him to pay back the money I had given him. I needed the money to buy a train ticket. He was furious and said he did not have any money. He told me to use my ATM card to buy a ticket.

I left in a fit of rage and went to the railway station. I had a little money left in my bank account. I had given all my savings to this 'rich' man. I inserted my ATM card into the ticket vending machine although I was not sure if it would work. I was glad to see the ticket emerge from the machine.

I kept looking towards the entrance as I waited for the train. My heart hoped that Ramesh would come to see me off. He did actually come in search of me. I dismissed my anger and disappointment and rushed to embrace him with tears welling in my eyes. 'I'll never abandon you,' he said and kissed my lips.

I returned to Germany feeling overjoyed. Once I reached Aachen, I went straight to Bilquis' room. I told her everything that happened without expecting her to understand. How could she, when I did not have a clear picture of my relationship with Ramesh myself?

21. The Magic of Hormones

I was unable to go to school or pay attention to my studies. There was nothing else on my mind but hormones and a longing to become a woman. I was considered to be the best student at school, but I discontinued my education after high school.

During this period, I met a man named Venu online. He was a university student who lived in London. Venu thought I was a woman, and we became friends. He was not outrageous like Ramesh and was polite when we spoke. He sent me sweets and gifts from London.

Ramesh called me when he was drunk and asked me to come to Paris and fought with me as usual. I told Venu about my love for Ramesh. When I spoke to Venu after a fight with Ramesh, I said that Ramesh was unfair and quarrelsome. Venu said that he liked me too and asked me to get rid of Ramesh. I refused to do this because I was deeply in love with Ramesh. Venu remained a good friend.

It was finally time to visit my new psychologist again. During the consultation, she said, 'I understand that you haven't lied about your problems.' She gave me a letter permitting me to consult a doctor who would prescribe hormones. Joy coursed through my veins.

At a major hospital in Aachen, I met the doctor who specialised in hormonal therapy. He took a sample of my blood and asked me to return the next day. The following morning there was a report on the doctor's table that contained information about the hormonal levels in my blood. The doctor injected Androcur into my abdomen. It would limit the production of male hormones in my body. He also prescribed hormone pills.

After that, I felt dead tired and slept for the rest of the day. I knew hormones have adverse side effects. Even after sleeping I felt exhausted and was only revived by the thought of getting rid of my male appearance and turning into a woman. I had my first hormone pill with devotion as if it were a divine offering.

I told my mother about the pills. She was anxious and said, 'Son, do anything you like but don't play with your body.' When my brother heard about it, he said with disdain, 'Are you going to completely turn into an ombodu?' I didn't care about what they said. My life was in those pills. There was magic in them.

My body temperature fluctuated because of the hormone pills and I always felt hungry. Within a month, I noticed changes in my body. My face acquired a more feminine appearance. My breasts blossomed and grew. My hips widened. I experienced everything that a woman would experience when she comes of age. I was filled with courage and hope. I began to wear women's clothes all the time.

Although I was happy, Ramesh always did something to ruin my happiness. He pestered me for money every day. He never talked about anything else. I gradually began to hate him. I befriended another man called Karan through the internet. He often asked me to meet him but I did not feel like it. Soon, I began avoiding him too.

A few days later, someone named Bala called me. He told me that a friend had given him my number. He said that he was twenty-eight and had recently married Selvi, who was good friends with my brother. After we spoke a few times, Bala spilled the truth. He was Karan's elder brother. He had taken my number from his cell phone.

I did not wish to conceal the fact that I was a transwoman. But when Bala heard it, he was shaken. I told him about transwomen and described my gradual transformation. He listened to me attentively. I then told him about Ramesh and that he was treating me like a slave and extorting money. Bala consoled me and encouraged me to leave him.

It was his friendship that gave me the courage to let go of Ramesh. I severed all ties with him. But I am still terrified that he may stab me if he sees me somewhere. Bala told Selvi about me and that I had become a transwoman. Selvi called me and asked what my brother thought of me. I told her, 'Anna hasn't accepted me and now he no longer talks about it.'

A day or two later, as we were talking, Bala said that he wanted something from me and asked me to promise him that I would give him what he wanted. 'If you don't accept my demand, I'll stop talking to you,' he said. I could not think of leaving Bala after all the love he had shown me. I decided I would give him anything he asked for.

'I want you to be my second wife' he blurted. I began to tremble in shock. 'But you have a wife…' I said, sobbing over the phone. Bala showered me with words of love. 'Had I met you before I met Selvi,' he told me, 'I would've married you.'

I dissolved in his love. He had convinced me with his words. Bala asked me to meet him at the Bonn railway station. I was hesitant but I wanted to meet him, and so I agreed.

22. The Brothers

The next day, I stole fifty euros from Appa's purse and went to meet Bala. I reached the Bonn railway station at 1 p.m. Bala was waiting for me at the parking lot. I got into his car and sat in the back. He remained sitting in the driver's seat. I noticed that he was shorter than me as well.

We began talking, and he told me that he was a videographer who filmed events like weddings. He showed me some of the movies he had made. Eventually, he asked me about my sexual relationship with Ramesh. I alluded to what had happened when I met Ramesh.

Bala held my hand and asked, 'Won't you make me happy by doing for me what you did for him?' I replied, 'I'm reluctant because you're married.' He got out of the car and came and sat next to me in the backseat. He hugged me and kissed my lips. I gradually succumbed to his advances.

It was very hot in the car. We were both drenched in sweat. I sucked his penis but he did not come. I finally said, 'I can't do this anymore.' That was when he came. He hugged me with satisfaction and said, 'I'll not abandon you. You must be my second wife.' I spent some more time with him before taking the train back to Aachen.

When I got off at the Aachen railway station, I called Angel and told her everything that had happened. She rebuked me and said, 'If he likes you so much, he can divorce his wife and live with you. These men just want to make us their concubines.' Although I completely agreed with what she said, I asked her, 'When their own families don't accept transwomen, how could they accept transwomen as their wives?' My stupidity only made Angel anxious.

I wondered how I could expect any respect from Bala when none of my lovers had treated me with any respect. It was my love for Bala that made me think like this. After our meeting, I developed a keen love for him. We called each other every day.

Bala promised me, 'I'll soon marry you in a secret ceremony.' He asked me not to chat with any other man on the phone or over the internet. I decided to be a chaste wife and was loyal to him. Bala laid down new conditions every day. One of them was not to dress up glamorously.

The second meeting took place the very next week. Bala arranged for us to meet at his home. He said that he would be alone once his wife left for work. I was scared to go to his place. But Bala convinced me with his words, the eloquent trickster that he was.

I reluctantly visited his house. He was in touch with many Tamil women and had recorded his sexual encounters with them without their knowledge. He showed me his recordings. I did not show any interest in seeing them and feared that he would record me as well.

We had sex in his bed. His dried wedding garlands were hanging in his bedroom. It had not even been three months since his wedding but the groom was ready to get married again. From what I know, wives are very intelligent and they somehow discover their husbands' secret affairs in no time. Selvi was one of those clever wives.

She knew I was friends with Karan too, so she called my brother and said, 'My husband and his brother are spoiling your innocent brother.' Although I was furious with her then, today I am grateful when I think of her. My family was shaken after hearing about my antics.

My brother broke my phone and yelled, 'When there are men from so many different communities in Germany, why do you have to be friends with Tamil men and put us to shame? If I get to know that you're dating Tamil men, I will throw you out of the house.'

I picked up the scattered parts of my phone and ran out of the house. When I reassembled the phone, it came back to life. I called Bala and anxiously told him everything that had happened. Bala said, 'Then let's not talk for a few days.' He stopped calling me after that. He did not answer my calls either.

I think he felt humiliated when people heard that he was dating a transwoman. I called Karan and told him everything that had happened. He responded by saying, 'I'm not like my brother. Do you know how much I love you?' His words were very comforting at that moment. 'I just want to be friends with you,' he said. I agreed.

I waited at a nearby railway station for Karan to pick me up in his car. We went to a neighbouring park and talked. As we were talking, he pinched my waist. I jumped in surprise. 'Did you get scared?' he asked. I told him, 'I'm in a relationship with your brother. I'm like your sister-in-law.'

He scratched his beard and began to think. I did not really believe what I had said. I asked him to drop me at the station. As we drove back, Karan began to caress my arms and thighs. Although I liked the bearded man's mischief, I suppressed my feelings because he was Bala's brother.

He stopped the car in front of the railway station and kissed my cheeks before leaving. As I tried to kiss him back, he suddenly grabbed my head and kissed me on my lips. I needed the bearded man's kiss at that moment. I wanted to be close to him. I did not get out of the car.

We drove off in search of an isolated place. After we found a suitable spot and parked, he sprang on me. I stopped him and asked, 'Is it enough if I suck your penis?' He unbuttoned his trousers and leaned back before I even finished the question. Before long, he came. I was possessed by guilt. I was in a relationship with his brother. I had betrayed Bala.

When I reached home, I anxiously called Angel and told her everything. She laughed and said, 'You've done nothing wrong! You don't need to feel guilty. Bala isn't your husband and he just used you to satisfy his desires.' But I still felt uneasy. I called him to tell him the truth but he did not answer my call.

I searched for his home number and called him. Selvi answered the call. Something compelled me to tell her everything. She was shocked to hear what I had to say. She warned me, 'Bala and his brother are misusing you. Stay away from them!'

Two days later Bala called me. He was furious and yelled, 'You can suck all the men in your city but don't meddle with my family and my life.' He called me names and then suddenly turned into a social activist by saying, 'Please don't ruin the lives of Tamil men and if you persist, you'll be suitably punished.' I retorted, 'I have been punished enough,' and hung up.

The end of my relationship with Bala made me sad. A part of me felt that I had lost a friendship because of a mistake I made. However, I comforted myself by resolving never to get deceived again. I decided that it was good that I had ended this relationship. The first thing I did after that was to change my phone number. My life moved on to another phase.

23. A Meeting of Transwomen

Turna organised a weekly meeting of transwomen from Aachen. Every Saturday, there were at least ten transwomen who attended the meeting at Turna's home. When I joined them, I noticed that everyone else who attended was white. As far as I know, German transwomen come out only after they turn thirty. Until then they suffer and struggle with their own identities.

Although we conversed and shared our experiences, there were certain things that I could not understand. For instance, some of them had been married to women and were now divorced. Some even had children. Some of the transwomen still had relationships with women. The oldest among us was Jenny, who was fifty-four. My journey to become a woman had begun when I was three, but Jenny had begun hers when she was forty. Most Indian transwomen think about wanting to become women when they are in their teens, but in Europe it happens when they are much older.

Could the relative absence of a rich culture of transwomen in Europe be a sociological reason for this delayed desire to change gender? There are mentions of transwomen in our ancient texts. This is how the *Tiruvenmpavai* venerates Lord Shiva: 'He shines forth as man, woman and ali [eunuch]; as the earth, the sky and other worlds...' The *Tiruvasakam* says Lord Shiva is 'the begetter of man, woman and ali...' But I do not know why none of the hundreds of modern Tamil poets have ever written love poems about transwomen.

I saw a surgically made vagina for the first time when I met a transwoman called Emila at the meetings. I do not know if the surgery was done well, but I saw her take a rubber penis and insert it into her vagina. The sight of her vagina only intensified my longing for surgery. I cannot deny that I was jealous of Emila.

Jenny treated me as her own daughter. Everyone at the transwomen meetings was generally concerned about me because I was the youngest among them. They asked me not to get addicted to weed and other drugs. However, I neither drank alcohol nor smoked at that time.

I was turning into a beautiful and attractive woman with the help of hormones. News of my transformation spread across Aachen as if it were the eighth wonder of the world. Lecherous men on the streets would look at me and ask without any hesitation, 'Shall we go to a bar?'

The Tamil men who drank with my father were worse. They would give my father some great suggestions like 'If I had a child like that, I would've euthanised him' or 'throw him out of the house'. Appa would come home and tell us this. He would throw things at me. People in our community started to say that I was a shame to those who had come from Yazhpanam. Some had spiritual opinions that I was a hybrid foetus born to my mother because of the sins she had committed.

I felt like leaving home. But where would I go? Without my family's protection, I would certainly be sexually assaulted and mistreated. It was better to be beaten up and confined to a corner of my family's house. Beatings and verbal abuse were not new to me. I was introduced to violence even before I was introduced to the alphabet.

My mother discovered a solution to all these problems. Her plan was to suppress my effeminacy, seduce a poor family from Sri Lanka with the promise of a life abroad and get me married to their daughter as soon as possible. She had decided to ruin an innocent woman's life along with mine. Although I was tempted to ask her to try to get me married to a good man, I could understand that wretched mothers have their own inconsistent ways of thinking. How could my mother understand my problems when even my psychologist could not entirely understand me?

I concluded that only education could secure a protected future for me. I would have to study well, look for a job, stand on my own feet and take care of myself. I applied to a college to complete my studies. As there were four months before the next academic year began, I decided to work at a restaurant. I really liked going to work dressed up as a woman.

Once, while browsing the internet, I chanced upon a video of transwomen organising a religious festival at a temple in a town called Kilang in Malaysia. I felt what one would feel if one were to witness the world of the gods. The Malaysian Tamil transwomen were adorned in all the ways that I had imagined adorning myself. They looked like divine apsaras wearing beautiful silk saris, pavadai and davani with fine makeup. Their hair was in long braids with their heads adorned with strings of jasmine flowers. I longed to establish a connection with them. I wanted to know more about that festival.

As I browsed further, I got to know that it was called the Bahuchara Mata festival. Bahuchara Mata is the goddess of transwomen. There is an ancient temple in Gujarat devoted to this goddess. A Tamil transwoman had built a similar temple in Malaysia. Transwomen celebrate this festival throughout the year at that temple.

On the festival website, there was an interview with two transwomen from Switzerland named Sundari and Ranjitha who were attending the festival. In the interview they said that they had moved to Europe in the 1980s and had worked as cabaret dancers. They were now married to white men and continued to live there. I immediately searched for them on Facebook and other social platforms, but I could not find them.

I found the email of the person who had published the interview and wrote to him, introducing myself as a Tamil transwoman. I included my phone number and asked for Ranjitha or Sundari's number. I received a call the very next day. A male voice said, 'Vanakkam! This is Sundari speaking.'

I introduced myself to Sundari Pati, 'I'm Thanuja, a transwoman from Sri Lanka. I live in Germany with my family.' Sundari was amazed as she had never met a transwoman from Sri Lanka. She told me that she was calling from Singapore. She said that she spends half the year in Singapore and the other half in Switzerland.

She asked me, 'Are you part of a *jamaat*, Thanuja?' I did not know what jamaat meant. She explained in fluent German that jamaat refers to a familial structure that exists among transwomen. An older transwoman adopts a younger transwoman, gives her love and support and becomes her mentor. This culture first emerged in north India and spread all across the country. Later, the system was established in Singapore and Malaysia by Tamil transwomen.

Before Sundari could finish her explanation, I asked her, 'Would you please accept me as your daughter?' She replied, 'You can be my granddaughter.' She said that I may call her 'pati', which meant 'grandmother' in Tamil. 'Tomorrow, I'll look for a good mother for you,' she said. Joy seemed to heal my bleeding heart. I was going to have new relationships. I was no longer alone!

Sundari Pati called me the next day. 'Vanakkam, Pati…' I began but she interrupted me. 'You first need to understand a few traditions,' she said. 'In our community, when young transwomen talk to their elders, they should first say, "*Pampadthi*, guru". It means, "I touch your feet and take your blessings." The elders in turn must say, "Be well" or "*Jiyo*".'

I later learnt that transwomen use many Sanskrit words because this culture emerged in India. Sundari Pati said, 'I've found a good mother for you.' She passed the phone to someone who was sitting beside her. The new voice said, 'Daughter.' Her voice penetrated my soul and brought tears to my eyes. I said 'Pampadthi' as I was told to. My new 'mother' said, 'Jiyo.' She said her name was Priya, and that I was to call her 'Priya Amma'. She lived in Switzerland. 'I have a lot to say to you, daughter,' she told me. 'I'll visit you when I return to Europe.'

I had finally found a mother and a mentor who would be close to me. She would hold my hand and guide me through the path of life. After I spoke to her, I visited her Facebook page and looked at her photos. She looked completely like a woman. I saw in her a resemblance to the movie actress Nadiya.

I would talk to Priya Amma every day over the phone. She taught me many strategies, tricks and ways to behave like a woman. I befriended many transwomen from Malaysia and Singapore through her Facebook page, including Sukanya and Buvana whom I had earlier seen in documentaries. These new relationships gave me courage. I was no longer alone in this merciless world!

24. The New Amma

During our conversations, Priya Amma told me her life story. She was born to a poor family in Malaysia. Her father was a prominent rowdy in Kuala Lumpur and her mother was a sex worker. Her two brothers were born to different fathers. When her father discovered her effeminacy, he gave her away to a woman known as Asha Pati, who ran a brothel. Priya would send a share of her earnings to her father every month.

When she turned eighteen, Priya moved to Singapore. There, she legally registered as a sex worker and worked in Singapore's red-light district. She sent money to her family in Malaysia. It was in Singapore that Priya met

Sundari, who soon arranged for her to emigrate to Switzerland.

Priya began her career as a sex worker in Europe on Lang Street, which is Zurich's red-light district. She was put under the care of two transwomen, Durga and Lalitha. These two transwomen appropriated all her earnings and then got her illegally married to a white man so that she could get a permanent Swiss visa. Over time, differences arose between Priya and her caretakers. Durga and Lalitha went to the extent of hiring men to attack Priya and threatened to expose her fake marriage to the Swiss government. Priya Amma told me that she still feared for her safety.

The day of our meeting finally arrived. Priya Amma sent me a message a few days after she returned from Singapore. She wanted to come to Aachen to meet me. That made me happy and anxious at the same time. I was miserable because I did not know where I could arrange for her to stay.

Finally, I told my mother that a friend of mine would be visiting from Switzerland and she would stay with us. Amma initially refused but I begged her and made her agree. Appa and my brother were not bothered. They had believed all their lives that I would become a man if I were to be close to a woman, so perhaps it was good news for them that I would be bringing a woman home.

A white man drove Priya Amma to our home and then immediately left. For the first time in my life, I saw a Tamil transwoman who had completely transitioned into a woman. I touched her feet and embraced her. My body trembled with emotion.

Priya Amma was neatly dressed in stylish clothes and looked like a European woman. But she looked darker than she did in her pictures. Her face and her feet did not have the same complexion. She had brought some gifts for me and my family.

According to transwoman culture, a transwoman must adopt another transwoman as her daughter by presenting her with a sari. A sari is related to a transwoman's identity and basic rights. The hardships and beatings we endured to wear a sari in public were not insignificant. When Priya Amma gave me a beautiful silk sari, my eyes filled with tears.

Contrary to what I had thought, I could not deceive my family. Within a few minutes of meeting Priya Amma, my family knew that she was a transwoman. Although Priya looked exactly like a woman, her voice gave her away. My family took care of her because she was our guest. But they occasionally stared at me. My heart raced as I hoped there would be no fights while Priya Amma was at our home. However, my father surprisingly opened his heart to her and they had a long conversation.

Later, when Priya Amma and I were alone, she said that her ex-lover was a Sri Lankan Tamil. That was when I remembered Ramesh telling me that his friend was living with a transwoman in Switzerland. That transwoman was indeed Priya. I learnt that he had stolen a lot of money from Priya Amma and disappeared.

I took Priya out to show her Aachen. As we walked, we occasionally heard someone whistling at us. Someone stopped their car and asked Priya Amma for her phone number. She was around thirty-five then but looked ten years younger. She had surgically implanted silicone breasts. There was silicone in her hips as well, because of which she could not sit or lie down for too long. She had also undergone plastic surgery on her face.

Priya Amma had her gender reassignment surgery done in Thailand. She described the process in great detail: her testicles had been removed and her penis had been surgically transformed into something that looked like a vagina. There was no trace of the penis after surgery. The newly formed vagina looked just like a natural vagina. It also had an opening for sex. One could experience an orgasm during sex because the head of the penis is used to make the clitoris.

Priya told me, 'In Thailand, even a boorish man can be turned into a beautiful woman.' She encouraged me to get my gender reassignment surgery done in Thailand. I really looked forward to that wonderful day. The purpose of my life would be fulfilled at that very moment! But I did not have enough money for the surgery.

Priya told me there was a way out. 'Let's go to Cologne and do sex work there. Once we have saved enough money, let's go to Thailand.' I instantly rejected her plan. I told her, 'I refuse to do sex work. I want to study well and get a job and live a moral life.' She understood my stance on the matter and did not insist further.

We spoke all night after we got back home. Priya Amma had many stories from Malaysia. There were a few boys whose transwoman friends urged them to turn into women and get silicone implants. However, in time they discovered their true gender identity and went back to being men and even got married to women. There are also some men who undergo sex reassignment surgeries to become women so that they can make money from sex work.

When I heard these stories from Priya, I realised that the legal restrictions in Germany for someone who wished to undergo gender reassignment surgery were justified. I believe a qualified psychologist's guidance is necessary for those who wish to undergo gender reassignment surgeries. Priya Amma told me that she earned up to a thousand Swiss francs a day from sex work and that none of her clients could tell that she was a transwoman.

It was unbelievable to me. I enthusiastically asked her, 'Is the gender reassignment surgery in Thailand done so well?' Seeing my enthusiasm, Priya asked me, 'Do you want to do it too?' I said 'yes' with irrepressible eagerness. Priya Amma took me to the bathroom and showed me her vagina. Her vagina looked so natural that even women would not be able to tell that she wasn't born with it.

Many Malaysian transwomen go to a particular hospital in Thailand to get the surgery done. They also undergo several plastic surgeries for their faces and bodies. Priya Amma would apply a cream to her face when she woke up in the morning. The skin on her face would peel when she applied it. She would peel the skin off her face and her face would appear radiant.

The real use of that cream was for removing burnt skin. It was made of powerful herbs and continuous use could even cause cancer. Priya Amma also knew that the liquid silicone implanted in her hips could be life-threatening. None of this bothered her. She only concerned herself with remaining fair and beautiful.

Priya told me that her guru lived in Mumbai. Her name was Tilakam. She too became my 'grandmother'. Tilakam's 'mother' was known as 'Bombay' Manjula. The traditions of transwomen in Malaysia and Singapore began with Manjula. She introduced the Indian jamaat system to the transwomen there. Three older transwomen of the region were chosen as the first 'mothers' and 'grandmothers' and their 'daughters' and 'granddaughters' continued the system in Malaysia and Singapore.

In the system, a daughter would have to give a share of her earnings to her mother. Priya Amma was still sending money to Tilakam Pati. Over time, many transwomen began to misuse this practice. They would brainwash younger transwomen and force them into sex work to extract money from them.

Priya Amma returned to Switzerland after a couple of days. During the time that I spent with her, I was not only very happy but also many things became clear to me. I understood that transwomen constantly face many challenges and difficulties in their lives. But I told myself that I must not fear these challenges because this is what I was born to be.

Once Priya left, my mother began her appeal to me. 'Did you look at her?' said Amma. 'She isn't peaceful; she doesn't sleep in peace. No matter how much makeup she applies, she can't conceal the deathly pallor on her face. She always looks as though she's lost something. Is this the life you want?' I tried to reassure her by saying, 'I'll not lose anything, Amma. I'll be a confident woman among these people.' But time was waiting with a cruel smile to show how difficult this would be.

When Priya next called me, I asked her to give up sex work. She asked me, 'Are you asking me to beg, daughter?' I asked her why she didn't get a job. 'That's what I'm doing,' she replied. She believed that in the transwomen community sex work was like a normal job. Her calls grew less frequent after that. I longed for her love but I could not have it.

Soon, Tilakam Pati called me from Mumbai and then Sundari Pati called me from Singapore. They pestered me to give up my studies and become a sex worker. I politely refused. They mocked me by saying, 'You're not a pottai. You're a fat bull of a man.' They called me names like *'dai'*, 'po da' and *'va da'*, which are used by transwomen to insult or berate each other. These words deeply hurt transwomen who wish to live like women.

I learnt that both these senior transwomen extracted money from younger transwomen, who were made to do sex work while the older ones lived lazy and ostentatious lives. If anyone refused to give them money, they would be threatened with expulsion from the jamaat. A transwoman who is no longer part of a jamaat cannot go to places frequented by other sex workers or attend meetings of transwomen. This threat allowed some transwomen to become dictators.

25. Group Discussion

One day, I received a phone call. The person who called did not introduce himself. He just said that someone had written terrible things about me on one of the Tamil diasporic websites and had uploaded some of my pictures there. Then the caller hung up. I anxiously looked for the website.

Indeed, there was a picture of me as a man next to a recent picture of me as a woman. The photos were accompanied by a slanderous article. When I looked at the pictures, I knew that it was my ex-lover Bala who had done this. I had emailed these pictures to him. Bala hurt me as he had said he would.

In the slanderous piece, Bala said that I was pretending to be a woman to seduce and deceive men and rob them of their money and that there were many men who had been deceived. The website, which had always been particular about upholding the integrity of the media and Tamil culture, used the pronoun 'he' and the term 'ali' to address me. I was utterly heartbroken.

The slander spread like wildfire to other Tamil websites and also Facebook. Even those who were close to me spread the news. I had been close to the Sri Lankan Tamil community from the time I was young. I had believed that our culture, practices and lives were superior to others. But over the next few days I understood that our practices were mere superstitions.

People did not even bother to find out if the information on the website was true before launching an indiscriminate attack against me. Young Tamil men who were born in Europe started a Facebook group called 'Kummalam' where they said nasty things about me. These 'heroes' wrote in broken Tamil that I should be beaten up and the greatest among them said that I should be shot for spoiling Tamil culture.

I called Bala and asked him, 'Why did you do this?' Bala said that it wasn't him. I knew that he was lying because he kept contradicting himself when he spoke. He tried to dismiss me by saying, 'Someone you deceived must have informed the website.' I cursed him and hung up.

I was furious. I went to the police and filed a complaint against the website for publishing a slanderous article. The police investigated the matter and then told me, 'The website is being run by someone in Britain. Our jurisdiction is limited to Germany. We cannot do anything.' I refused to let it go. I would not spare the website even if it were being run on the moon.

There was a London number on that website. I called that number in a fit of irrepressible rage. I heard a male voice say 'Vanakkam' in beautiful Tamil. I said, 'My name's Thanujan. You've published a fake article about me.' He responded, 'Oh, is that you?' I exploded. 'First, learn to give respect,' I yelled. 'I'm a transwoman. What evidence do you have in support of this article?' He replied, 'We took several days to investigate the matter and discovered the truth about you.'

With a raging heart I retorted, 'Damn your investigations! I've never taken money from any man. On the contrary, it's Tamil men who have misused me and taken money from me. You've laid accusations on me and published this article. If the men of Germany beat me or ask me to sleep with them after reading this article, you're responsible for that. If you don't remove this fake news and my photographs from the website now, I'll commit suicide. I'll record my own suicide, which you can then proudly publish on your website.' I disconnected the call after ending my rant.

The man called me back right away and pleaded, 'Don't act in haste. I'll remove the article from the website.' The article was gone from the website within thirty minutes. But it was too late. The damage had already been done and I had already become infamous among the Tamil community of Europe. I was lucky that my brother was on a trip to India at the time. It meant that I could be spared his beatings for a while.

I had earlier made a friend called Rohan through Facebook. We called each other now and then. He did not know that I was a transwoman. Now he called and asked me, 'Are you really an ali?' I angrily replied, 'People like you will never understand what I say. You're all perverted!' I hung up. After that, I disappeared from the internet and avoided Tamil people.

People from other countries were not any better. Following my friend Bilquis' suggestion, I created an account on a dating website. That is how I met Ameen, a Moroccan who lived in Germany. When we spoke over the phone, I did not tell him that I was a transwoman. I wondered how long I could keep the truth from him, but I feared he would leave me if I told him the truth.

Ameen said that he wanted to meet me. But I was hesitant. If he saw me, he might identify me as a transwoman. However, the more I refused to meet him, the crazier he became for me. I introduced Bilquis to Ameen, but she revealed to him that I was a transwoman. He called me and asked furiously, 'Are you a transwoman? Your friend says you're deceiving me!' I was shocked and lied, 'I am a real woman. I think Bilquis lied to you because she's jealous of me.' He seemed to somewhat believe me. After I handled the situation with Ameen, I called Bilquis. 'What did you tell Ameen about me?' I asked in rage. She simply responded, 'I didn't lie.' Then she abruptly ended the call. Even seers cannot tell us what can make people jealous.

I was determined to make Ameen fully believe that I was a woman. This was the way to teach Bilquis a lesson. I forgot everything that Bilquis had done for me and became petty. I was possessed by a desire to seek revenge and insult my friend by walking hand in hand with Ameen. But it was I who ended up learning a lesson.

I told Ameen that I would meet him. I was working at a restaurant at the time and finished work at 8 p.m. Ameen told me that he would pick me up from the restaurant after work. He travelled a long distance to meet me. I was wearing a T-shirt and jeans and had taken great care with my makeup. After I got into his car, he sped away and didn't stop until we were in an isolated area surrounded by cornfields somewhere on the outskirts of the city.

As we were talking in the car, Ameen tried to kiss me. I did not let him because I was afraid that he would feel the hair on my cheeks and jaw. Also, my sex drive had diminished ever since I began taking hormones. I no longer looked for sex everywhere and was only attracted to people I was fond of. I did not find Ameen attractive.

From the moment we met, I could sense that Ameen was determined to have sex. He did not utter a word of love; instead, he held me with his strong hands and made me lean back. He tore my blouse in a frenzy and bit my breasts. He behaved like a madman. I sank into the car seat, powerless to resist. I felt his teeth on my neck.

He fumbled as he brought out his penis and shoved it into my mouth. I was afraid that he would tear my jeans next. If he discovered that I was a transwoman, this lust-driven madman might kill me. As I pretended to suck his penis, I tried to think. Even if I screamed and wept, there was no one around who could come to my help. I would have to be strategic to escape.

I pretended to gasp and narrowed my eyes as if I was going to faint. My pretence was effective. He withdrew in fear and asked, 'What happened?' I panted and said, 'I have asthma. It's difficult to breathe in the car. I need to step out for some fresh air.' He immediately opened the door. The moment I stepped out of the car I began to run away. I was barefoot but entered the cornfield. My legs were soon smeared in mud as I ran for dear life.

Ameen did not run after me. I heard his car leave. Once I had crossed the field and reached a street, I walked home. I was scared that he would be hiding somewhere on the way. But I reached home and washed off the mud in the bathroom. Later, I looked at my phone. There were several calls from Ameen.

I called him back. I thought he would be angry, but he began to sob. 'I've never been like this with any woman,' he said. 'I don't know what came over me today.' I very calmly said, 'Ameen, you're crazy. Consult a good doctor. Stay away from me!' Then I hung up and thought about what had happened. I knew that he might have killed me if I had not managed to escape.

I had never felt so scared while dressed in men's clothing. But since I began to dress in women's clothes, I've always felt scared. Transwomen live with the constant fear of being beaten or murdered. If a transwoman is raped, to whom can she complain? If she complains, she would be asked 'What were you doing in women's clothes?' or 'Why did you go alone to a place like that?' and she would be blamed for what happened.

The police in every country treat transwomen like criminals. I have never heard of feminist organisations or political movements protesting against sexual assaults on transwomen. They seem to think that the term 'sexual crime' does not apply to transwomen. Have you ever seen a report in the media or even on social media about a sexual crime committed against a transwoman?

I only told my friend Angel about the sexual assaults I had suffered. I thought that only another transwoman would understand me. Such incidents happen in every transwoman's life. I did not go to work for the next two days because I was scared that Ameen would come in search of me. When I did go back to work, my employer asked me to leave.

26. The Chariot Festival

There is a chariot festival that is celebrated with great fanfare at the Shri Amman temple in Hamm. Millions of devotees from various parts of Germany and elsewhere visit the temple for this festival. I too wanted to attend the festival. Although there were rumours and tales about me circulating among the Tamils of Germany, I still decided to go dressed as a woman.

The festival was on a Saturday. I went to my white friend Elvis's place to change my clothes. I wore the beautiful sari Priya Amma had given me, did my makeup, styled my hair and wore anklets that jingled when I walked. Elvis and I took a train to the festival.

There was a surging crowd as people thronged towards the temple. The sound of auspicious music and the joyous cries of people merged into one. Devotees once carried bird *kavadi*s on their backs at this temple. But the police banned that practice after the beam of a bird kavadi broke. I saw people dancing with milk and paneer kavadis on their backs. Women walked with pots of burning coal on their heads.

My sari rustled and my anklets jingled as I enthusiastically walked among the crowd. Perhaps the resident deity did not approve of my enthusiasm, because I soon heard people behind me muttering 'Mohana'. That was the name I was known by on the website that had spread rumours about me and in the Tamil chat group. There were more cries of 'ali' and 'ombodu'.

I knew this would happen, so I was not really bothered by these taunts. I held Elvis's hand as we circumambulated the temple. We prayed and then walked towards the market. I thought I saw an inauspicious sign as we entered the market. There was a strange-looking man who was staring at me. He had brown hair and wore several earrings. His goatee had been dyed brown like his hair. I walked past him, but his strange appearance remained in my mind's eye.

I saw some of the Tamil people who lived in Aachen at the market. Some of them recognised me and we exchanged greetings. The others were shocked into silence to see me dressed as a woman. We wandered around for a while before deciding to walk back to the train station to take the train back to Aachen.

There were some young Tamil men standing by the station entrance. They cried 'ombodu' when they saw me. Elvis was furious when she realised that they were insulting me. She was ready to pick a fight. I restrained her and pulled her inside the station. I heard an old man in the Tamil group say, 'That's the one from the website.'

I struggled to control myself, but I also feared that I might be beaten up if I protested. We Tamils are known for attacking in groups. I had seen people in Tamil Nadu and Colombo being thoroughly beaten up by mobs. But when I later recollected everything that had happened that day, I felt proud. I had achieved my first victory by wearing women's clothes while walking past a brainless, uncultured and inhuman group of people.

The day after the chariot festival, someone named Satish called me. He introduced himself as a friend of my 'Facebook friend' Rohan. 'I got your number from Rohan,' he revealed. Satish knew that I was a transwoman thanks to the gossipy website. He told me that he had lived in Germany for a long time and was now living in Holland because of some visa issues.

Satish seemed to be an expert in the subtle art of seducing a woman with his words, because he took my breath away with his romantic statements. We were soon speaking day and night over the phone as if it were our only source of bliss. After a while, I told him that I wanted to see his face. He sent me a photo of himself. It was the young man with the goatee who was staring at me at the chariot festival!

Satish said, 'When I saw you at the festival, I fell in love with you.' I thought that the gods had finally taken mercy on me. We eventually met in Dartmouth one afternoon. Satish and I sat in a park near the railway station. Although he looked boorish, he was refined in the way he spoke and carried himself. He was effusive in his expressions of love. I began to believe with all my heart that he was the man I had been looking for.

It was a little chilly that afternoon; he removed his jacket and covered me with it. I do not remember who hugged whom first. Our bodies entwined as we kissed each other's lips. I felt deep love in his touch and embrace. After some time, we left the park and went to the station. But I was unable to let go of him. My eyes were welling with tears at the thought of saying goodbye. He gave me a deep kiss and saw me off.

I spent my time longing to see him again. Our phone conversations somewhat helped suppress my desire. Satish asked me to come to Holland. Aachen was not very far from the Dutch border. I told my mother that I was going to visit a white woman friend and took a train to Holland. I sat down in the comfort of my seat and shut my eyes. My heart directed the train as it sped ahead.

27. Holland

Ganistan, a friend of Satish's, was waiting for me at the railway station. When he saw me, he said, 'Anni, Vanakkam.' I was overjoyed when I heard that. He told me he was twenty-two, but he looked like a sixteen-year-old. He even had the personality of a young boy. He drove me to Satish's house.

Holland was a very beautiful country. Satish's house was in the middle of a lush and peaceful meadow. There were five or six rooms in the house, and six young men were living with Satish. None of them had a regular job. They made a living by indulging in rowdy behaviour, stealing and gambling. My to-be lover was the leader of the gang.

Everyone in his house knew that I was a transwoman. They acknowledged me as his lover and called me 'anni'. I had longed for such love and approval. Satish had done what no other man I knew had ever done for me—he openly said that I was his lover. At that very moment, I became his wife in my heart of hearts.

One of the bedrooms had been reserved for me. I kept my bag in that room. Satish made dinner. He seemed to be an expert cook. After a delicious meal, I sat on my bed lost in thought. I had not told Satish that I was yet to have gender reassignment surgery. Priya Amma had taught me how to deceive men even without having undergone surgery by concealing my penis to give the man the impression that he was penetrating a vagina. I was convinced that this strategy would never fail me.

Satish came to my room a little while later. He did not behave like a desperate man. I leaned my head on his chest and talked to him. He was an eloquent speaker. Talking to him made me feel better than all the counselling I had undergone. I felt very peaceful. It seemed like a blessing to be with him. I was the one who initiated sex.

Once I had him under my control, I whispered in his ear, 'My gender reassignment surgery wasn't done well. I don't want to show you my vagina. I will get it fixed soon.' Instead of making me feel miserable about it, he simply accepted what I said. I sucked his penis and gave him an orgasm.

We spoke late into the night before he left to see his friends. I wanted to hold him all night. But my wish was never fulfilled during the week that I spent with him. Satish spent more time with his friends than he did with me. He did not sleep in my room.

I would wake up early in the morning and lock myself in the bathroom, feeling disgusted and furious whenever I looked at my penis. I would have been free and happy with my boyfriend if not for this wretched thing! I would shave my face repeatedly and then carefully shave the hair on my arms and legs.

After my bath, Satish would come and dry my hair before combing it. His friends would tease us but he would remain unfazed. He even did my makeup, finishing by marking my forehead with a small spot of kumkum. He wanted me to look like a married woman.

One day, Ganistan was fighting with his girlfriend over the phone. Satish intervened and tried to appease the girl. That night, Satish told me about her. She was a rich Tamil divorcee. Ganistan's love for her was just a pretence to get her money. He had already deceived her several times and taken a lot of her money.

All his friends were a part of the plot. They told the woman that Ganistan had consumed poison and fleeced her by asking her to pay for his treatment. I told Satish that it's wrong to play with a woman's life. In response, Satish slandered her sexual reputation. I thought that there was no guarantee that they would not do the same thing to me!

The next day, I pulled Ganistan aside and reprimanded him. He was annoyed that Satish had told me everything and began to accuse him of deceiving me. 'Do you think no one has betrayed you?' Ganistan said.

'Satish is in love with a married woman. She lives in Dartmouth, and he often visits her. He doesn't love you. He wants to marry you just to get a permanent German visa.'

I felt distressed and was not sure if I should believe him. I remembered that Satish met me for the first time in Dartmouth. I ran to him. 'Do you have another lover?' I asked. At first, he tried to be evasive. When I told him what Ganistan had said, he finally admitted the truth.

'But I truly love you with all my heart,' he quickly added. 'I don't intend to use you to get a visa. Ganistan is making stuff up because he's high on weed. I'll definitely marry you. I swear!' He kept trying to reassure me. I began to believe him.

I became worried about Satish's girlfriend. I thought I must somehow make them break up. Satish was my life's only hope. His support gave me immeasurable peace. I must not lose him! I had become part of a love triangle because I wanted to be the only person he loved. I had had enough of being a mistress.

Satish's girlfriend was a cis woman. As a transwoman, it made me feel inferior. My inferiority gave rise to jealousy, which gave rise to rage. I began to fight a lot with Satish. He tried very hard to placate me. Once, he left the house after a fight. He returned an hour later and took me to a church.

At the entrance to the church, he asked me to face east as he brought out a tali from his pocket. The tali had an S-shaped pendant that he tied around my neck. When he made three knots, tears began to stream down my face. I shut my eyes and prayed that he would never leave me. He took some kumkum out of his shirt pocket and made a mark on my forehead. From that very moment I was Satish's wife! This is what I had been waiting for!

I kept gazing at the yellow thread. I pressed it against my eyes. A progressive woman would mock such traditional practices, but I really liked all these customs. Transwomen will hold on to anything that makes them feel like a complete woman!

Satish said, 'When I get money, I'll buy you a tali made of gold.' I refused his offer. The authenticity of a yellow thread was missing in a showy tali made of gold. Besides, it would be hard to conceal a gold tali. When we returned home, Satish's friends were astonished to see the kumkum on my forehead, 'You're already married!' they exclaimed. I shyly hid behind Satish.

I had to return to Germany as college would soon reopen. I also had to look for a part-time job. But I did not have the heart to leave Satish. However, he promised me that he would soon come to see me in Germany.

28. The Fortune of being Married

When I returned home, I considered myself to be a newly married woman with a tali around my neck. I carefully concealed the tali under my clothes. But Amma somehow noticed and asked, 'What's this new fashion?' She asked me to get rid of it. I did not respond. She went away muttering something.

My mother did not really care that I was wearing a tali or that I had returned after a week. She had absolutely no respect for me or anything that I did. She did not consider me one of her children. But I did not care that Amma and I had grown apart. I was so deeply in love! I thought my husband would be a mother and a father to me.

On the day after I returned to Germany, Satish called me from Dartmouth. He asked me to meet him there. I asked him, 'Have you come to meet your girlfriend in Dartmouth?'

'Yes, I need to talk to her about a few things,' he said. I replied, 'In that case, I'll not come to see you.'

He did not beg me to come. Instead, he asked me to lend him two hundred euros. I was blinded by my love for my 'husband' and told myself that he would somehow let go of his girlfriend. I transferred the money to his account. Then I frantically looked for a part-time job in Aachen.

After a while, I got another call from Satish. This time he asked me to come to Rotterdam. He was staying there with his friends. I took a train there. My husband was waiting for me at the station. He took me to his friends' home. Shortly after we arrived, his friends went out. It was just the two of us in the house.

Satish passionately embraced me. He was very happy to see that I was wearing the tali that he had given me. We had some satisfying sex and then began talking. He told me that he wanted to raise a family with me but he could not get a job or start a business because of some issues with his visa. He asked, 'Shall we register our marriage?'

If he was legally married to someone like me who had a permanent visa, he would get a permanent German visa as well. I believed that he would never abandon me if we got married. I agreed to register our marriage. He thanked me and we kissed. We tearfully parted at the railway station. I did not know that it would be the last time I would see him.

I began to read up on German marriage laws. I called the relevant offices and got answers to my questions. As I was nineteen, age was not a problem. A transwoman was not forbidden from marrying a man. But we would have to wait at least six months after submitting the necessary documents.

However, my 'husband' could not wait for six months. He found a new Tamil girlfriend in Norway. My last phone conversation with him still feels like a wound in my heart. He told me that he was going to Norway. I was angry and bitter. I asked him, 'What are you going to do with me?' He responded by saying, 'I tied a tali around your neck. Isn't that enough?'

I began to hate Satish with all my heart. Even I was a little astonished at how much hatred I felt for him. I ended the call and went to the bathroom. I looked at the tali on my neck in the mirror. Then I removed it. I cannot tell you how painful it was. I felt like a worm at that moment.

Even her mother would not be bothered by this transwoman's cries. No one is going to ensure that I get justice. I would be declared guilty in every case.

29. My First Glass of Alcohol

I got a part-time job at a restaurant before college reopened. My job was to wash dishes. Now I could pay for my own education. I no longer had to pester my mother or steal money from my father. I went to college in women's clothes. I requested my teacher not to tell my fellow students that I'm a transwoman. Although she gave me a wide-eyed look, she agreed to my request.

I began to pay attention to my studies. Angel and Rose encouraged me to study well. Although I was determined to study seriously, would not someone my age be occasionally eager to meet her friends and chat with them? One of my Facebook friends, a man named Prem, asked me to visit him in Dartmouth. I agreed, and we arranged to meet one Saturday evening.

Prem was waiting for me along with his friends Roshan, Yut and Roshan's girlfriend Kartika, who was around eighteen. They all knew that I was a transwoman. Our conversations were mostly about transgender people. They asked me many questions about the topic, which I answered as best I could.

We went to a nearby disco in the evening. Kartika had drinks with the men. That was the first time I saw a Tamil woman drinking alcohol. My new friends asked me to have a drink as well. It was my first experience of alcohol. Although I did not like the taste, I liked the feeling of excitement that it gave me.

I went to the dance floor and began to dance. Many men came and danced with me. They could not tell that I was a transwoman. Some of them asked me for my phone number. It was a joyful night. Early the next morning, my friends drove me to the railway station and I took a train back to Aachen.

I decided that I liked this group of friends. I met them every Saturday evening. We spent our time happily talking and dancing at the disco. Yut thought that he had the right to be close to me. He indirectly asked me to have sex with him. But I was not attracted to him.

Prem was the oldest among us and gave me a lot of advice. He suggested that I stop dating Tamil men and date white men instead. 'They are the only ones who'll respect you,' he said. But he did not know that white men do not respect transwomen either.

We celebrated New Year's Eve 2012 at a disco in Essen. Kartika's friend Sukanya lived there, and she came out with us too. There was another group of Tamils at the disco. Someone named Guna from the group asked me for my number. He called me the next day and wished me a Happy New Year. It started the next chapter of my life.

30. Love and War

Guna and I often called each other. His words helped me get rid of my loneliness. However, I did not tell him that I'm a transwoman. Guna did not approve of me drinking alcohol. He asked me how a woman who was so devoted to Tamil culture could drink. I justified myself by telling him about my life's miseries and the many men who had deceived me.

Guna was five years older than me. He had been part of the Liberation Tigers movement and was deeply devoted to the liberation of Tamil Eezham. However, he had to flee Sri Lanka during the last war in 2009 and had resettled in Germany as a refugee. Guna told me, 'Your suffering is nothing compared to what our people had to suffer during the war.' Those words were oddly comforting.

Guna worked at a restaurant and sent money to his parents, who were still in Sri Lanka. He would call me on holidays and talk to me while he drank alcohol. When I asked him why he drank so much, he replied, 'I drink to forget the wounds that were inflicted by the war and the thousands of corpses that I have seen.'

As the days went by, I began to like him more. There was something very dignified about the way he spoke. I did not meet my disco friends as often and in fact did not step out of the house unless I had to. I would spend my evenings talking to Guna.

A month after we began talking, Guna began to express his love for me. But I was hesitant to reciprocate because I did not know how to tell him that I was a transwoman. We began to have fights because I had not reacted the way he had hoped.

Guna would drink more and feel remorseful about everything that he had said. He hurt me by saying, 'You didn't accept my love because I can't speak fluent German like you. I'm not beautiful like you and I don't have a permanent visa.' The wounds he inflicted provoked me to say the truth.

Over the next half an hour I told him everything. Guna patiently listened and then said, 'Even if you're a transwoman, you're a woman. Let us adopt a child from Sri Lanka.' Nothing in the world could have made me happier. I began to love Guna with all my heart.

I went to meet Guna in Frankfurt one Saturday. We met at the railway station. Guna had a majestic personality, but he had a childlike face. I noticed that he was taller than me. He embraced me and gave me a bouquet of flowers. It was the first time a man had given me flowers. We hired a car from the station and drove to his home.

Guna lived in an apartment on the outskirts of Frankfurt. It was already 10 p.m. by the time we arrived. Once we went inside, I saw that there were cigarette stubs and empty bottles lying everywhere. After dinner, as we talked, Guna began to caress me. It made me feel very emotional, and I hugged him. We kissed and then he carried me to his bedroom. We undressed. As always, I had tucked my penis between my thighs and worn tight underwear. I had not told Guna that I was yet to undergo gender reassignment surgery. I began to feel anxious that he would hate me if he saw my penis. He began playing with my budding breasts. 'Do you like them?' I asked. He nodded.

Guna placed his hand on my waist. I held his hand and said, 'Not now. I'm yet to get my surgery done. Only after that will I have a beautiful vagina.' Guna was clearly disappointed. I sucked his penis to make him feel better. As always, I was scared of losing a man because I did not please him in bed. I was happy with his love and affection and in return I gave him a lot of pleasure.

I returned home the following evening. After that, I called Guna every day. I soon found that he was short-tempered. He would get furious over trifles. We began to have fights, but would usually reconcile by the next day. I began spending most of my weekends with Guna.

At college, my teacher was caring and did not discriminate against me for being a transwoman. When my female classmates would talk about their boyfriends, I would tell them about Guna with pride. But on days when I fought with him, I could not focus on my studies. I was unable to understand why Guna was constantly fighting with me.

Although we deeply loved each other, I could not give him the sexual pleasure that cis women could give him. I thought that was why he was growing hostile. The only solution was for me to become a complete woman. That was also my life's aim anyway.

I implored my psychologist to give me a letter allowing me to undergo gender reassignment surgery. She accepted my request as it had been a year since I had first consulted her. I sent my counsellor's recommendation letter to my medical insurance company hoping that they would take care of the expenses.

Unfortunately, two months later, I received a rejection letter from the company. There were some legal conditions that I had not yet fulfilled. The country's laws were like the doors of a fort. They stood between me and my goal. But I continued to try. Nearly every day I searched for information, made calls and filled out application forms.

My fights with Guna became more frequent. We often screamed at each other over the phone. I tried my best to control my anger, but I once swore at him. He said, 'You don't talk like a domestic woman. I don't want you.' He hung up. I was deeply hurt. My throat felt like it had split into two.

I called him back to ask him to forgive me, but he did not answer my calls. I grew very bitter. I heated a knife on the stove and burnt my arm with it. Guna eventually called me back after a couple of days and we reconciled. The wound that my words had inflicted on him had healed, but the scar from the burn on my arm still exists.

By then, my family had accepted that they could never change me. There was no point in beating a twenty-year-old. Even if they threw me out, I would survive. My parents began to put up with me because they had no choice. My brother tried to be more patient with me.

31. I Knocked and the Doors Opened

It was June 2012 when I finally received the letter that gave me permission to undergo gender reassignment surgery. Perhaps you can imagine the joy I felt when I read the letter from the medical insurance company. I felt as though flowers had blossomed all over my body.

I did not waste a second. I had already prepared a list of all the doctors who perform sex reassignment surgeries in Germany. I chose a doctor named Oscur, who was of Turkish descent. He was recommended by transwomen who had been his patients. The hospital where he worked was in Cologne.

One would have to wait for months for other doctors. But Dr Oscur would perform the surgery within a week. However, some of my friends warned me that there were flaws in his surgery. The vaginas he created were not deep enough.

During gender reassignment surgery, the penis is severed, and its skin is used to create the vagina. As most transwomen generally have small penises, there was not enough skin and the vaginas that were created were not deep enough. But this did not bother me. I had to become a complete woman as soon as possible. I had waited long enough!

I called Dr Oscur on a Friday. He asked me to come to his office on Monday. My sister visited us from Switzerland that weekend. I told her that I was going to meet the doctor. She asked me for the details and then fell silent for a little while. Then she said that she would accompany me to the doctor.

My sister and I visited Dr Oscur on Monday. He was a sweet middle-aged man. He patiently explained the procedure to us and asked us if we had any questions. 'I have no questions,' I said. 'Perform the surgery today if possible and make me a woman!' The doctor smiled and said, 'It's rare to see someone as young as you come for this procedure. Most of the people who come here are above thirty-five. You don't look like a transwoman. You have a naturally feminine voice. Allah has created a woman.'

The doctor's words gave me self-confidence and joy. My sister took my hand in hers. Dr Oscur told us, 'I can only create an artificial vagina. I cannot guarantee that you will feel anything or experience pleasure when you're having sex. You will never fully experience the sexual pleasure that a woman experiences.' I calmly replied, 'What I will feel after this surgery is something that a woman can never experience. No woman or transwoman can experience what I have experienced during sex. Sensations differ from person to person.'

The doctor smiled and said, 'What you say is right. But it's my responsibility to warn you.' He told us that there are people who undergo the surgery and later want their penises back.

The doctor took me to an adjoining room and asked me to lie down. After examining my penis, he said that he could create a vagina with a depth of only about twelve centimetres. This was because I had a small penis. He warned me that I might feel uncomfortable during sex if the man's penis is large. But I was not worried at all about the discomfort. I was desperate to get the surgery done.

Dr Oscur showed me pictures of surgeries that he had done before. The artificial vaginas he created looked like real ones. However, I had only seen vaginas in pornographic movies, so I thought I should ask my sister for her opinion. We went back to the doctor's office and I showed her the pictures. She looked at them and said to Dr Oscur, 'You're a truly great artist!'

Next, a sample of my blood was taken for some tests. After about four hours, they told me that I was healthy and ready for gender reassignment surgery. My surgery was scheduled for the following week.

That evening, we had dinner together as a family because my sister was visiting. She told everyone that my surgery was scheduled for next week. Amma said, 'Why didn't you tell us earlier?' I replied, 'You have never helped me with anything. What's the point of telling you?' Amma made a final attempt to change my mind. 'You can wear female clothes and take hormones,' she said. 'But please don't have the surgery. You wouldn't be able to become a man again even if you wanted to.'

I could only feel sad that my mother still did not understand me even after all these years. The dishes were in a state of disarray on the table as our arguments grew. My sister supported me and said that the times had changed based on what she knew about European laws. The conversation ended with my parents still not supporting my decision. However, they did not try to stop me either. But the most shocking thing was that my brother had become supportive. He told me he would drive me to the hospital on the day of the surgery.

I called Guna that day and told him about the surgery. He conveyed his best wishes and told me that he would visit me at the hospital. I then informed Priya Amma and Sundari Pati. They expressed their joy at the news. Sundari was in Singapore, but Priya was in Europe. However, she did not say anything about visiting me. I would have been happy if a transwoman was present during the surgery because gender reassignment surgery is a holy ritual for us. It is like a new birth!

My teacher at college granted me a week's leave before the surgery. The week passed by like a dream as I waited for the day of my nirvanam.

PART II

32. The Holy Nirvanam

My big day was 18 June! My siblings dropped me off at the hospital the evening before. I had a room to myself. It had a television and a private toilet. I was asked not to eat after 7 p.m. Through the window, I could see the beautiful dome of the church that was at the heart of Cologne. I looked at it for a long time. It reminded me of the time in Madurai when I implored Jesus Christ to turn me into a woman. I felt relieved now that I had my family's support. I did not know when I fell asleep that night.

I woke up early in the morning, bathed and got ready. The nurse entered my room at 7 a.m. and gave me some medicine. I was asked to remove my clothes and wait. I did as I was told and covered myself with a blanket. A little while later, a male nurse entered and wheeled me to the operating theatre.

To put me under anaesthesia, they inserted a needle in my tailbone. As I grew unconscious I thought I heard Dr Oscur's voice. His voice sounded like my mother's voice but addled. I heard the rustle of palm leaves. That is all I remember.

When I woke up after the surgery, I felt exhausted and nauseous. I sat up with the nurse's help and vomited into a cup. I could not see my new vagina yet. An hour later, they took me to my room to recuperate. A little later, my mother and siblings entered the room. I welcomed them with a weak smile and told them that the surgery was a success.

Amma had brought me some food. I was very hungry and instantly began to eat. My family stayed with me for nearly two hours. A few minutes after they left,

I vomited everything I had eaten. The nurse told me that it was the effect of the anaesthesia.

My uncle and aunt called from Switzerland to ask how I was doing. Some other relatives called me as well. When Sundari Pati called, she began singing on the phone. 'A new girl has been born!' she declared. Priya Amma told me that she had lit a lamp in the temple and prayed for me. She gave me suggestions to recover. After she asked me to drink a lot of water, I always kept a bottle of water near me.

Kamini, a transwoman from Malaysia, was my chithi according to transwoman practice. She messaged me on Facebook saying that she was visiting Germany and asked me to get in touch with her. I called her and said, 'My nirvanam is done, Chithi … I'm in the hospital.' She congratulated me and asked me to meet her after I recovered.

I slept early that night because I was exhausted. However, I woke up in pain. I called the nurse because the pain was unbearable. She gave me some painkillers, which allowed me to sleep.

I felt better the next morning after breakfast. The doctor examined me and left. My stomach felt swollen because I had not defecated for three days. But I controlled myself because I was scared to get up and walk to the toilet. However, the nurse suggested that I go and relieve myself.

I slowly got up but felt dizzy and collapsed back onto my bed. The nurse came to my aid. I held her hand and walked to the toilet. I had to hold my breath and apply pressure as I tried to defecate which made me urinate through my stitches rather than the tube that had been inserted. I shuddered in pain as if someone had splashed hot water on me and yelled for the nurse.

She gave me some cotton and asked me to wet it and wipe myself with it. That was when I saw my new vagina for the first time. My vagina was swollen and covered with stitches. It looked terrible. But I was overjoyed to see it.

The irritation subsided once I washed myself. The nurse helped me bathe because I was unable to stand straight. Dr Oscur examined me in the afternoon. He told me that he had inserted some cotton in the opening that had been created and that it would be replaced the next day.

The next day I was taken to Dr Oscur's room. There were a male and a female nurse on duty to assist the doctor. He made me sit on a tall chair and spread my legs. The male nurse tightly held my arms. The doctor removed the long cotton roll that had been inserted inside my vagina. I felt a slight pain.

When it was removed, blood oozed out of the opening. The female nurse held a circular mirror in front of my vagina so that I could see what the doctor was going to do. I would have to do this by myself once I was back home.

The doctor spread my vagina open with a slim pair of pliers. I trembled, unable to bear the pain. He took some cotton with another pair of pliers, dipped it in antiseptic and then inserted it inside my vagina by slowly turning it. I screamed in pain.

After thoroughly disinfecting my vagina, he inserted a fresh roll of cotton into it. I would have to keep some cotton inside my vagina for two weeks to ensure that it does not close. There was blood dripping from my vagina. The chair was wet with my blood. I told myself that it was my menstrual blood.

My family, friends and relatives often visited me during my stay in the hospital. On a visit with my mother and aunt, my sister lifted my blanket and looked at my vagina. 'Amma, this looks so real,' she said. Amma and my aunt were too embarrassed to take a look at my vagina. But they looked happy.

It took a week before I was able to slowly walk around the hospital. Dr Oscur playfully said to me, 'You're very beautiful. There are many doctors who have their eyes on you.' I spoke to many people around the hospital. None of them could tell that I was a transwoman.

Guna visited me as well. We were meeting after a long time. I noticed that there was a swelling on his neck. When I touched it, it felt like goitre. I asked him what it was, but he just said that it was nothing. He spent two hours with me. I was very comforted by his visit.

When it was time for him to leave, I begged him to stay a bit longer. But he left. I went with him to the entrance and saw him off. I thought about the terrible fight we had the last time he left me. I went back to my room and silently cried. My body ached even when I cried.

I remained in the hospital for a couple of weeks, but the tube that had been inserted so I could urinate had not been removed even after I got back home. Dr Oscur had given me an artificial penis, antiseptic and a lubricating cream that would ease the penis into my vagina. I was instructed to repeatedly insert the penis into my vagina for at least an hour every day. That would give my vagina the right shape.

Once I was formally discharged from the hospital, I took a train back home. The pain in my vagina lingered during the journey. When I reached home, Amma warmly welcomed me with a smiling face. She helped me lie down and then went to the pharmacy with my prescription to buy everything I needed.

When I urinated, I felt a slight irritation. I endured it, but the pain increased. I could not pee the next day. The pain became unbearable. Amma took me to a nearby hospital. After examining me, they said that I had a urinary infection. The tube had caused the infection. After taking the medicines I was given, I went back home with my mother. I could fall asleep after that.

The next day, Amma cleaned my vagina with antiseptic. She asked me what the artificial penis was for, so I told her what the doctor had asked me to do. But I trembled when I thought of the pain I had felt when the penis had been inserted inside my vagina. Amma comforted me and tried to help. But when she inserted the plastic penis inside my vagina, I screamed in pain. I began to bleed profusely. Blood kept oozing from my vagina and spreading all over my thighs. I clenched my abdomen and tried to control the pain. Amma burst out crying as she held the blood-drenched penis in her hand. She cried out to Nallur Kandan, Lourda Matha and Vellaikadarkarai Sufi. I called Guna and wept.

I cried myself to sleep that night. The next day, we went back to Dr Oscur. I was again made to sit on the tall chair. The tube that had been inserted inside me was removed first. The doctor examined my vagina and said that it was very narrow. He asked me to insert the artificial penis into my vagina more frequently.

After that, I began to insert it regularly. I would lock myself in the bedroom, apply some lubrication inside my vagina and slowly insert and remove the penis. Although I felt some initial discomfort, the pain gradually subsided. I did this every day for half an hour.

After a month, the swelling had completely disappeared. My vagina looked very beautiful. I went to Cologne to meet the doctor for the last time. Guna had the day off, so he accompanied me. Dr Oscur examined me and said, 'Your vagina looks good now. The opening is wide enough.'

I suppressed my shyness and asked, 'When can I have sex?' The doctor smiled and said, 'You can start from today.' I profusely thanked him from the bottom of my heart and left feeling elated. Guna and I went to a Chinese restaurant to celebrate. Then we booked a room in a nearby hotel. We lay in bed kissing and hugging each other. 'Won't it be risky for you to have sex?' Guna asked. I laughed and said, 'No.'

Guna removed my underwear. The doctor had inserted some cotton inside after cleaning my vagina. Guna was scared when he saw the bloodstained cotton. I tried to reassure him but Guna refused to have sex. 'Your health is what matters to me,' he declared. He kissed me lovingly. Then we went back to our respective cities.

33. Kamini Chithi

Whenever I looked at my new body, I would be ecstatic. I would tell my imaginary friends, 'I no longer have to conceal my penis between my legs. I can wear anything I like. I no longer feel ashamed to have sex.' I was now a complete woman. After all the humiliations, obstacles and pain, I had finally asserted my identity.

To share my joy with another transwoman, I went to Dartmouth to meet Kamini Chithi. She was living with her German lover. I touched her feet and she embraced me. 'You look like an angel,' she said and kissed my forehead. Kamini was a flawless beauty as well. Her lover did not know that she was a transwoman. They had met when he was travelling through Malaysia. He was a sweet man who was very friendly with me. He had put up Kamini's photographs all over the house and had hung her anklets around a doll's neck. It was clear that he was crazy about her.

Kamini Chithi gave me a beautiful red sari. The material was see-through and the blouse was sleeveless. It looked like the saris that Bollywood actresses wore. I was embarrassed and said, 'I'm too shy to wear this sari.' Kamini held my face and looked into my eyes. 'Thanuja! This is how you must dress from now on,' she cried. 'You're very beautiful. Get rid of needless shame and insecurity!'

Later, she took a look at my vagina and said, 'He's made it well.' Every minute I spent with Kamini Chithi filled me with enthusiasm and courage. I left for home feeling happy.

I went to Guna's place on the weekend. The swelling in his neck had increased. I insisted on taking him to the doctor. Guna was diagnosed with tuberculosis. The doctor said it was caused by his heavy smoking and the unclean environment in his house. He recommended immediate hospitalisation.

However, Guna initially refused treatment. He was scared he would lose his job if he had to undergo long treatment. I somehow convinced him to get the surgery done. The goitre in his neck was removed and his neck was bandaged. However, he was always in a bad mood and angry with me. Perhaps it was because of the painful surgery.

There were still a few days left until college reopened, so I was able to stay in Guna's house while he was in the hospital. I cleaned every inch of the place. I visited him in the hospital every day and took care of him. I pretended that I was his wife and took care of him with all my heart.

Guna's Turkish friends from work would visit him in the hospital. They would praise my beauty and tease Guna. One evening, once visiting hours had ended, one of the Turkish men drove me from the hospital to Guna's home. The next day I found out that Guna did not like that I had accepted a ride from another man. When he saw me, he yelled at me despite the pain in his neck. 'You're not a Tamil woman!' he shouted.

Guna grew increasingly suspicious of me for no reason. He kept repeating the same phrase: 'You're not a Tamil woman.' He even began to ask me, 'Didn't you sleep with anyone last night?' I realised that he did not feel even a fraction of the love that I felt for him.

We spent our days fighting and accusing each other of imaginary wrongs. When Guna recovered and returned to his home, I went back to mine. I had gone there with a heart full of love and returned with a wounded heart. The wounds separated us like a moat.

34. Manjal Neerattu

The ritual that is performed for transwomen forty days after their gender reassignment surgery is the same one that is performed for girls who have come of age. It is called *'Manjal Neerattu'*, a ritual bathing ceremony. The transwoman bathes in turmeric water, wears a new sari and worships the goddess Santhoshi Mata. The transwoman mother has to organise this ritual for her daughters.

A prayer ceremony should be performed before the surgery as well, but my transwoman mother did not do that for me. That is why Priya Amma wanted to organise the Manjal Neerattu. She asked me to visit her in Zurich. Sundari Pati would be there too. The thought of the fortieth-day ritual made me cry with joy.

Priya Amma was waiting for me at the Zurich railway station. I ran to her and took her blessings. She embraced me and gave me sweets. I noticed that she had lost weight. She looked even younger than she did before.

Her apartment was a twenty-minute walk from the station. After we arrived, Sundari Pati called and said she would visit the next day. Priya Amma and I cooked together and then ate, chatting all the while. Later, we slept on the same bed.

Early the next morning, she began to prepare for the ritual. She garlanded the photograph of Santhoshi Mata and then added rose water and turmeric to some water. Once everything was done, we went to the railway station and waited for Sundari Pati.

She emerged from the train looking resplendent in her beautiful silk sari and gold jewellery. She had kumkum on her forehead. I touched her feet, and she blessed me. Then she looked at me closely before turning to Priya Amma and saying, 'Take good care of her!' On the walk home, the two of them constantly cracked jokes and made me laugh.

It was time for the ritual. I sat naked in the bathroom as they smeared turmeric and sandalwood paste all over my body. First Priya Amma and then Sundari Pati poured turmeric water on my head. 'I hope you see a lot of success in your life as a woman, my daughter!' said Priya Amma as she blessed me. We then performed a prayer ceremony.

Priya Amma had made some delicious biryani for lunch. We had a wonderful lunch while chatting. However, I soon noticed that Sundari Pati had a habit of mocking people and talking behind their backs.

When we began talking about Kamini Chithi, Sundari said, 'Does she look like a woman? She is tall like a man and has a swagger.' I was disappointed to hear these kinds of comments.

After a while, it was time for Sundari Pati to go home. She was living with her Swiss lover, who was a retired police officer. We saw her off at the station. That night, Priya Amma told me many stories about Sundari Pati. What she said was not very nice. According to Priya, Sundari had stolen money to send Priya to Switzerland. Since then, she had been extorting money from Priya Amma.

Sundari Pati invited us over to her lover's house. During the day we spent with her, she often said something on a whim that would hurt us. We went shopping, and Sundari made Priya buy her many different kinds of bangles and perfumes. She bought whatever she liked with Priya Amma's money.

Priya was not the only one being extorted by Sundari Pati. There were many other transwomen who had been forced into sex work and Sundari was profiting from them. It seemed to me that all she did was insult others and live off their money. Priya Amma told me that Sundari Pati's lover knew nothing about any of this. She said that he would have Sundari arrested if he ever found out.

However, Priya was herself not aware of her legal rights in Switzerland. She was uneducated because she had been compelled to do sex work since she was young. The fake marriage she had registered to obtain a Swiss visa had cost her 40,000 francs. She would still have to give Sundari Pati and Tilakam Pati a share of the money she made from sex work.

This kind of thing happens everywhere in the transwomen community. There are many older transwomen who take advantage of helpless and innocent younger members of their community by trafficking them into sex work. There are many transwomen who are trapped in this system like bonded labourers.

I had spent all my savings for my trip to Zurich and Sundari Pati had appropriated whatever money Priya Amma had left. To raise some quick cash, Priya decided to invite one of her old clients over. But I was very sad that she had no option but to do sex work. I wrung my hands not knowing what to do.

An old man who was about seven feet tall arrived with a bottle of whiskey in his hand. Priya Amma called him 'the Horseman' because he owned a horse farm. She told him that I was her younger sister who was visiting from Malaysia. The old man grinned and tried to hug me, but Priya stopped him. 'She's not a sex worker,' she told him clearly.

The Horseman gave Amma 500 francs. He gave me 200 francs as a gift and asked me to watch them have sex. I initially said no. But Priya begged me to agree. The old man began with his games. Although he was grotesque, Priya pleasured him with her fine acting. I teared up as I watched my angel-like Priya Amma being crushed under his weight.

Once the old man was done, I gave him a towel and he went to have a shower. Later, we sat together and drank the alcohol he had brought. He left after some time. Once he was gone, Priya said, 'Don't worry, daughter. Our problems will soon be over.'

Although Priya Amma had a touchscreen phone, she did not know how to use it properly. She did not even know how to send an email. I was patiently showing her how to use the phone when Guna called me. He immediately thundered, 'Why haven't you returned to Germany?'

I explained that Priya Amma had asked me to spend a few days with her. Guna began to swear at me. As always, I threw the phone away and began crying. Priya consoled me by saying, 'Don't worry about anything … a thousand men will desire you for your beauty!'

35. The One Night Stand

Later, Priya Amma and I went out to a Tamil restaurant in Zurich. A young Tamil man at the table next to ours tried to talk to me. Priya asked him, 'What do you want?' He pointed to me and said, 'I like this woman.' Priya asked for his number.

After we were back home, she asked me to call him. When I did, the man asked, 'Will you come to the disco with me tonight?' He said that I could bring my friend along if I liked and that he would bring a friend too in that case. He was referring to Priya Amma.

That night, Priya and I wore flamboyant clothes and makeup like Bollywood actresses. We stood at the end of the lane that led to Priya's house and waited for the young man and his friend to pick us up in their car. When they arrived, we saw that both men looked handsome and refined.

On our way to the disco, the man was effusive about my beauty. He said that he liked me the moment he saw me. By the time we arrived, Priya Amma had gotten close to the other man. At the disco, the men were generous and bought us several drinks. Priya and I were soon truly drunk. My new friend and I kissed each other as we sipped our drinks.

At about 5 a.m., Priya Amma invited the men home. My partner and I took the bed while Priya and the other man lay on a bedsheet she spread on the floor. My partner kissed me all over my body and said loving things. I did not feel guilty that I was betraying Guna. I do not know why.

I had gone to the bathroom to lubricate my vagina before we began, but the man was unable to insert his penis into my vagina because he was not fully erect. A general practice among transwomen is that we stop giving blowjobs once we have our gender reassignment surgeries because we prefer vaginal sex. So I told him that I was not responsible for his flaccid penis. The man left feeling disappointed.

We did not keep in touch after that encounter. It remained a one-night stand. Soon, I returned to Germany with all the gifts and clothes that Priya Amma had given me. Not only had I received her love, but I had also learnt a few new lessons.

36. Ceaseless Struggle

My phone fights with Guna grew more frequent. I was determined to put an end to it. I called him and said, 'My love for you has diminished. I had sex with someone else when I was in Switzerland.' Guna initially did not believe me. 'You'd never do something like that,' he said. I replied, 'You hurt me every day because you suspected that I would do something like that. Now, I've done it, and it's all over.' I hung up.

The summer vacations ended, and college reopened. I started my last year of college. My class teacher was the only one there who knew that I had undergone gender reassignment surgery. She asked me if the wounds from the surgery had healed. I replied, 'My wounds have healed but when I laugh hard, I'm unable to control my impulse to pee.' She laughed and said, 'That is a woman's problem.'

Now that my surgery was done, I could legally change my gender to 'female' and also change my name. I submitted the required forms to make the changes along with a medical certificate, but my application was rejected. It was because I was still a Sri Lankan citizen. I was told that only transwomen who are German citizens can legally change their gender.

The law astonished me. It stated that foreign transwomen living in Germany can legally change their gender only if they are from countries that do not allow them to change their gender. My application was rejected because Sri Lanka had laws that allowed transwomen to change their gender.

The Sri Lankan consulate was in Frankfurt. I got in touch with them without further ado. The consulate officers confirmed that Sri Lankan transwomen are acknowledged as women on their identity cards and passports. I was not only overjoyed but also a little proud of my country.

I followed the consulate's instructions to apply for the change. First, I would have to get my documents and medical certificate translated into English. It cost 400 euros, which was quite expensive for me. When everything was done, I went to the Sri Lankan consulate with my documents.

However, the consulate was a little confused about the rules. They told me that I was the first transwoman to submit an application for a gender change. I noted that all the officers in the consulate were Sinhala. But they were not prejudiced, and they did not disregard my application. They reassured me that they would help me in any way they could.

I received a call from them a week later. They informed me that unfortunately I would have to go to Sri Lanka to change my name and gender as they did not have the authority to do it here. It was a big disappointment for me and my hopes were dashed.

My last hope now was to get German citizenship. I submitted the necessary documents. They told me that I would be granted citizenship if all the documents were in order. If they let me become a citizen, I could finally legally become a woman.

37. Rohan

I had cut off my Facebook friend Rohan after he called me with an insulting question when the slanderous piece about me was published on that Tamil website. However, he got in touch with me after a while and told me that he was going through a heartbreak. I did not have anyone to talk to at the time after my own breakup with Guna.

So, Rohan and I began calling each other every day. He gradually filled the void that Guna had left. Rohan lived in a town called Breda in the Netherlands. Once, he invited me to a small party at his friend's home. I was eager to meet Rohan, so I took a train to Breda.

Rohan was waiting at the station with his friends. The house they took me to had several hot dishes ready on the table and a stock of different kinds of alcoholic drinks. There were five men at the party, and I was the only woman. Rohan had reserved a bedroom upstairs for me.

Apparently, Rohan had still not recovered from his heartbreak. He looked depressed and kept smoking one cigarette after another. For someone who had opened his heart to me over the phone, he was distant. I was all the more irritated when he nonchalantly poured me a drink, so I adopted a strategy to attract him.

I began dancing closely with his friends. Rohan looked up to see me remove my blouse and dance in my bra. He was a little alarmed as he walked up to me and said, 'You're drunk.' He made me put my blouse back on. I was happy to finally have his attention. He dragged me upstairs to my bedroom and shut the door behind us.

I looked at him. He hugged me, stroked my cheeks and muttered, 'I love you.' Then he lifted my face and kissed me. I melted like dew and surrendered to him. He kissed me and we undressed each other. He lowered his face and licked my vagina. This was a new experience. The satisfaction of having become a woman gave me more joy than his tongue.

I took out the lubricant from my purse and smeared some in my vagina. Rohan struggled to insert his erect penis into my vagina. I did not know where to place my legs. The opening to my vagina was not straight—it curved a little inside. If I rested my legs on the bed, a flap of skin would shut the opening. We tried many times before we discovered that if I raised my legs, my vagina would open. But even then it was not easy for Rohan to penetrate me. He slowly inserted his penis inside. When he was about halfway in, he began to thrust. I felt an intense pain, as if I had been stabbed by a sharp knife.

I thought of the struggles, humiliation and torture I had to experience to finally arrive at this moment. I began to cry when I remembered being beaten by my family, the several men who used me for their sexual pleasure and betrayed me and the times when I was ridiculed in school. Rohan wiped my tears as he continued to penetrate me. He muttered again and again, 'I love you.'

When he touched the depths of my vagina, I was aroused and began to bite him. The pain in my vagina increased the faster he moved. I endured the pain to give him pleasure. I screamed silently in joy. 'This is femininity,' I said to myself. 'This pain is pleasure. This is what I had longed for. I've become a complete woman. I've won.' When we were finished, I lay in bed like a princess who had been blessed with all the honours in the world.

I was unable to walk straight the next morning. My vagina was swollen like a balloon. I made sure Rohan did not see it. After breakfast, Rohan took me to the station. I took a train back to Germany. Although I was very happy with what had happened the previous night, I was not in love with Rohan. I was not sure why. But I still liked him.

I called Priya Amma and Kamini Chithi. I was happy to share my first sexual experience after the surgery. My face had blossomed like a screw pine flower. But the snake of sorrow was waiting to enter the flower.

38. Towards Zurich

I grew increasingly stressed because there was no response to my application for citizenship. My gender and name remained the same as before for all official matters. When people looked at my passport in any office they would ask, 'Is this your brother's photograph?' I had no choice but to say, 'It is me, I'm a transwoman.' I could feel humiliation spread and grow all over me like moss.

I would graduate from college in a few months and would have to look for a job before that. If people saw my documents that declared I was a man with a male name, they would know that I am a transwoman. Who would employ a transwoman? I was also anxious to get a job that was related to what I had studied. All my earlier jobs were undocumented and temporary and I had only been paid a meagre salary.

I stopped going to college as my anxiety grew into a mental disorder. Instead, I went to Zurich to visit Priya Amma. She had just returned from Malaysia and brought silk saris and makeup for me. We gossiped and chatted with men online. They would be attracted by our beauty and we would be seduced by their words. This was our chief pastime when we were at home.

In the evenings, we would walk through the city. It was during one of these walks that we ran into Mona, Priya Amma's friend from Singapore. Mona was Chinese and around fifty-five years old. She worked at a hair salon. Mona invited us to her home. We bought some drinks and went over to Mona's place.

According to transwoman tradition, Mona was my 'grandmother'. She lived with Rati, a Tamil transwoman from Singapore who was around fifty but looked like she was thirty. She was also like a grandmother to me. She told me that when she was young, she had participated in a transwoman beauty contest and won the second prize.

Mona and Rati chain-smoked and drank like fish. Like Sundari Pati, they were taken to Switzerland in the 1980s to work as cabaret dancers at nightclubs. Rati told me that there were more than twenty transwomen from Singapore and Malaysia living in Switzerland. There were other groups that lived in various European countries. Most of them made a living doing sex work.

There were few transwomen who escaped sex work like Mona had. She had been a sex worker until she was forty but then enrolled herself in a hairstyling course and looked for a job. But Rati still struggled as a sex worker. Mona described to me the challenges and exploitation of sex workers.

She held my hand and said, 'You're lucky because you didn't have to struggle a lot to become a woman since you live in Europe. But our lives aren't like that. We had to suck thousands of cocks to save money for the surgery. Although we moved to Europe, we had to sell ourselves to take care of our families because we were born poor. We had to cosy up to every customer like kittens. We had to bark like dogs at every broker. Everyone sucked us dry. Now we walk around with withered bodies and dead hearts.'

On another day, Priya Amma took me to meet a transwoman named Sheela. She kept talking about her on our way there. Sheela had also come to Europe to do sex work. She was known as 'the Queen of Lang Street' because she had been beautiful when she was young. Her apartment was close to Lang Street.

But when I saw her, she did not seem to be the beauty that Priya Amma had said she was. She looked like a desiccated fish—or a dirty sack. It seemed like she had not bathed for days and had tied her hair in a topknot like a hermit. Her eyes revealed without a doubt that she was under the influence of drugs.

We touched her feet and she blessed us. 'Who's she, Priya?' she asked. 'Has she come from Malaysia to make money?' Priya shook her head. 'No, she is my daughter, a Sri Lankan Tamil who is a student.' Sheela could not believe it. Astonished, she asked me, 'Are there transwomen in Sri Lanka?' She was only convinced when she heard me speak in Eezham Tamil.

I felt sad when I saw Sheela. She sounded like someone who was mentally disturbed. The Queen of Lang Street sat like a mummy that had risen from her grave. We gave her some money and left.

39. Guru Mona

Once Mona invited me to go out. I wore beautiful clothes and went to her place. She was astonished to see my beauty and cautioned me, 'Listen, Thanuja! You're very beautiful. Don't do anything that will ruin your beauty. Never get silicone implants. Don't enlarge your breasts like Priya did. If you do this, your natural beauty will fade. Please don't destroy your beauty!' I agreed to do as she said.

We went to a piano bar. It was frequented by rich people. The price of alcohol there was very expensive. No matter how hard I tried in places like that, I was somehow possessed by a sense of inferiority. I went to sit in a dimly lit corner, but Mona made me sit at the centre of the bar. We drank some wine. Mona told me, 'Thanuja, first, get rid of your inferiority complex! You're more beautiful than Priya. There are thousands of men waiting for your eyes to beckon them.'

However, I felt that my breasts had not grown large enough. I was not satisfied with my figure. Priya Amma had surgically altered her body. When I told Mona my thoughts, she smiled and said, 'Who wants those silicon bags? Men like women with natural bodies like yours. Your problem is you keep running like a bridled horse! When you walk you must look at men's eyes and not at the ground!'

Mona told me that men admire me. 'They gaze at you in the streets, in shops and in this bar as well,' she declared. 'But you are like an innocent schoolgirl who doesn't pay attention. You need to make men come to you with your eyes. Your look is what gives them the permission to approach you!'

Without further ado, I tested what Mona said. I looked at a middle-aged white man who was talking to his friends. He let his eyes wander until he returned my look. After exchanging a few glances, the man came over and said to me, 'You're very beautiful.' It was exactly as Mona had said.

I do not remember his name now, but I do remember that he was the manager of a football club. He was smitten by my words and beauty. Not only did he pay our bill, but he was also generous enough to buy us some more drinks just to get close to me. He must have spent thousands of francs on us at the bar. Later, the man drove us home and even gave me his number.

'You're smart, Thanuja!' Mona said to me once we were home. 'You did what I asked you to do. Priya won't teach you all this. She wants you to always live in her shadow. She wants to rule over you.' She told me that her housemate Rati was also like that. 'She thinks that she is a queen simply because she is beautiful,' said Mona of Rati. 'But no queen does sex work. If you're beautiful, you should use your beauty in the best possible way. One mustn't wait in the streets for customers who will pay you fifty or a hundred francs.'

Mona said that Tamil transwomen were very beautiful and that white men fell for our chocolate skin. That was an unforgettable evening when Mona's great advice sculpted my mind and heart. I still use all the subtle tricks that Mona taught me. She was a great guru!

40. The Disco and Tamil Men

There were many discos that surrounded the red-light district in Zurich. Priya Amma told me that an Eezham Tamil was organising a party at one of those discos. I wanted to go, because I still liked the company of young Tamil men the most. I accompanied Priya, Mona and their white friend Thomas to the disco. Thomas stayed close to me and bought me several drinks. Priya Amma whispered, 'Daughter, he's stinking rich. Don't let go of him.'

But I was not interested in Thomas. My eyes were focused on the Tamil men there. I ignored Thomas, who was trying to dance with me. Mona quickly took Thomas's hand and they left together. I was not surprised to see the anger in Mona's sunken eyes when she looked at me. But it did not affect me because I was drunk. Priya and I were in a state of drunken ecstasy, and we remained at the disco. As we danced away, some Tamil men joined us in our furious dance. They began to caress and pinch us.

The ecstatic dance soon turned into assault. Two of the men suddenly pushed me against the wall. One of them kissed me without my consent while the other aggressively wormed his way through my dress and caressed my vagina, which was annoying. I struggled and managed to push them aside. I grabbed Priya's hand and dragged her out of the disco.

Outside, another group of Tamil men surrounded us. One of them grabbed my arms. I was unable to free myself from his grasp. Priya was drunk and unable to even stand upright. As I struggled to free myself, someone said in chaste Tamil, 'Do you only like white men's cocks?' I angrily replied, 'Yes, they're bigger.' He unzipped his trousers and showed me his penis.

He chuckled, 'Don't you like this one?' Eight to ten hands began to touch me when I screamed.

A white woman saw what was happening through her apartment window above. When I screamed, she threw a tub of yoghurt at the men. They in turn threw beer bottles at her window. The window cracked and the woman screamed. This shook Priya Amma to her senses. She began to struggle with the young men and tried to free me.

Just as things were getting desperate, we heard a police siren. The police arrived and arrested the young men who were harassing us. They were taken away in a van. The police did not ask me or Priya anything. She and I walked to the next street.

We saw many transwomen from Brazil, Somalia, Thailand and the Philippines there. They were sex workers waiting for customers. Priya also used to do sex work there so she knew most of them. We felt safe once we entered that street.

41. Getting to Know Myself

I again learnt many lessons on my trip to Switzerland. One was the difficulty in anticipating the dangers faced by transwomen. It was necessary for transwomen to keep their bodies and minds alert all the time. Only we could protect ourselves.

After I returned home, my family acted normally with me. It was a big relief. I called Rohan but only told him parts of what I did in Zurich. I kept many things from him. 'Don't ever leave me,' he said. I thought about that. I wished to have a permanent relationship with someone who respected me and treated me as his equal. I believed that life would give me peace, protection and joy.

Rohan and I began meeting every weekend in Aachen or Holland. We were only two hours away from each other. We would book a hotel room, have drinks and then have thrilling sex. Sometimes we would make love ten times a day. If I drank too much and vomited, he would wipe my mouth and put me to bed.

It took me a long time to understand my own body after I got my new vagina. During the surgery, the end of my penis was used to make something that resembled a clitoris. My frequent sexual encounters with Rohan helped me discover my new body's feelings. I would have orgasms whenever his penis or tongue stimulated my clitoris. I understood the true meaning of sexual pleasure only when I was twenty-one.

I was soon madly in love with Rohan. He would bring me gifts whenever we met and accompany me everywhere. His words that glowed with love made me radiant. He made me understand my own body. What more did I need? I forgot about everything else in this world and even began to distance myself from the transwomen community now that I had the life I needed. My relationship with them diminished. I began to believe that I was born a woman.

To have a fulfilling romantic life it is necessary to have more than just a good heart—one also needs money. I began to look for a job again. I remembered a childhood desire to be a flight attendant when I saw an advertisement for one such position online. It was with a well-known German airline, so I applied. But I did not tell them that I was a transwoman, and did not include copies of my passport and identity card.

Within a few weeks, I received a letter for an in-person interview. At the interview, they tested my knowledge of English among other things. I was very confident and did well. My interviewers congratulated me and said that I would be appointed as a trainee. They asked me to send them my documents including my passport. I left feeling happy but hesitant.

Once I returned home, I sent them a note along with my documents that said, 'I'm a transwoman. I have had my gender reassignment surgery. I'm waiting to get my name and gender changed.' They called me within the next two days and said, 'There are many women who apply to us. Since you're not as qualified as they are, you haven't been selected.'

They were lying. It was clear that I was rejected despite passing all the tests because I was a transwoman. How could they evaluate me and ciswomen by the same standard? I have spent my entire life struggling to become a woman. My struggles have made me stronger and more experienced than an ordinary woman.

Being rejected for my body has been the greatest injustice. My gender is as natural as the sky. Nature cannot be punished! I temporarily let go of my desire to become a flight attendant and looked for an agent who would get me a different job. Luckily there was a vacancy in a cosmetics factory near my home.

This time when I submitted my documents, I did not conceal the fact that I was a transwoman. The agent responded, 'Alright, you look and sound like a woman. Don't let anyone in the factory know that you're a transwoman.' I told him that I wouldn't want to reveal myself even if I was asked to.

Work at the factory began at 6 a.m. I made sure I behaved like a woman to avert suspicion. I had an easy job in which I had to supervise a small machine that produced skin cream. If something went wrong with the production chain, I had to stop the machine and resolve the issue.

Although I soon made a few friends at my new job, I would be hurt when they commented on the dark colour of my skin. Men pursued me here as well. They would ogle at me during the break and ask me for my number. I would shut their mouths by saying, 'I have a boyfriend.'

I liked my new job. I was paid 1,200 euros a month. I would give 300 euros to my mother for my family's expenses and saved some money every month for a laser treatment that would remove facial hair and make my face look smooth. I spent the rest of the money as I wished.

Rohan and I decided that we would get married and adopt a child after I became a German citizen and changed my gender. Rohan placed a golden ring on my finger and promised never to let go of me. I really do not remember how many men have made such promises to me. But I fully trusted Rohan. His love made me blossom every day.

I did not have a secret relationship with any other man because I was completely in love with Rohan and had faith in him. I stopped going to discos. Rohan was the only man with whom I drank. All I did was go to work and spend my weekends in a hotel with Rohan. We did not fight much.

Through our passion, we turned sex into an art. Despite developing fissures and wounds in my vagina every time he penetrated me, I continued to have sex with him. When we were together, we never looked at our phones. While I was with him, I would forget all my worries.

My family was amazed to see the rapid transformation of my body in such a short while. I had developed a completely female body. Most transwomen become beautiful after their sex reassignment surgeries not merely because of the change to their bodies but also because one of the secrets to their beauty lies in their hearts which are now filled with joy.

42. The Star Actresses

It was again time for the annual chariot festival at the temple in Hamm. Kamini Chithi had just returned from her holiday in Malaysia and was in Dartmouth. She asked me if I wanted to go to the festival with her. I asked Rohan to come along too, but for some reason he was not interested. He said that Kamini and I should go ahead without him.

I took the earliest train to Kamini Chithi's place on the day of the festival. Her partner presented me with a copy of a flight attendant's autobiography. Kamini had bought me a beautiful black and blue pavadai and davani from Malaysia. I decided to wear those clothes for the festival.

After braiding my long hair, I decorated it with jasmine flowers. Kamini did my makeup. She wore a light blue Kanchipuram silk sari and looked resplendent. It was as though she was wearing the sky. The makeup, jewellery and clothes we wore would put any movie star to shame.

The railway station at Hamm was full of Tamil devotees. The Tamil women there were stunned to see us. We suddenly felt like stars because some of them even took selfies with us. I think that they did not realise that we were transwomen because they did not ask us anything. There were more eyes looking at us than the goddess at the festival!

There were many people I knew who were also at the festival. Some who had avoided me the last time I attended were now eager to speak to me. Many people even asked me for my phone number, and some followed me. But I avoided them. After all, I had my loving Rohan.

I would suddenly take a day off from work to visit Rohan. I did not care much for my job because I was sure I would soon become a German citizen. Based on my performance in the airline interview, I already knew that I could become a flight attendant. I thought that once I had officially changed my gender and name I would easily find a similar job.

I told my mother about Rohan. I ensured that there was no one but Amma at home when I invited Rohan over and introduced them to each other. Amma seemed to like him. Later, I introduced him to my sister over the phone. They soon became friends.

On the days when I went to meet Rohan, Amma began giving me some food she had made for him. I was happy to see Rohan and my family grow closer. But Rohan's family knew nothing about me. They only knew that he was in love with a woman from Germany.

Several months later, there was still no response to my application for citizenship. I grew impatient and called the office for an update. They asked me if I was working now. When I said yes, they told me to send them the contract. I did as I was told. This time, I received a quick response. They told me that my contract was only for six months, but to become a citizen, I would need an open-ended contract or documents to show that I am a student. I anxiously rushed to the agent who got me the job at the factory and told him my predicament. He was a kind man who said that he would give me a permanent contract after the six-month period. That meant that in two months I could get the document that I needed.

43. An Independent House

Every time Rohan and I met, we would spend several hundred euros on the hotel room. We decided that we should move in together into a rented house in Aachen. After spending several days looking for the right place, we found a beautiful apartment. Rohan left his factory job in Holland to be with me.

He did not have any savings, so I bought furniture and other things for our new home with a 5,000-euro loan. My mother and brother gave me some money to help furnish the new flat. They began to support me because they believed that my joy was theirs. My rebelliousness and perseverance had paid off; I had succeeded in making my family understand me. I was happy to have succeeded in making them understand me at a time when other transwomen were being ostracised by their families.

I managed to get Rohan a job at a restaurant. Everything went well for about two weeks, but then things took an unexpected turn. I noticed that Rohan was gradually getting tired of living with me. He would get furious at the smallest of things. I would retaliate because I had become arrogant living in my own flat.

Eventually, Rohan stopped going to work because he did not know the local language well. He started complaining about everything and began to insinuate that he wanted to go back to Holland. I feared that he would abandon me and leave me in debt.

His parents believed that he was living with his girlfriend in Germany. I had talked to his mother a few times over the phone. His mother would always say, 'Make him learn from his mistakes and take care of him.' However, once I casually mentioned that my family lives in Aachen. That 'clue' was enough for her.

She inquired about me and discovered that I am a transwoman. After that, his family immediately began trying to separate us.

After I got back from work one evening, Rohan said that he wanted to talk to me. He told me that his parents were forcing him to get married to his uncle's daughter who lives in Sri Lanka. I controlled my tears and asked him, 'What have you decided?' He told me that he would go back to Holland to convince his parents about us. I did not think that it would work, but I didn't know what else we could do.

The next day, I called Rohan many times during my break at work but he did not answer my calls. I was anxious that something had happened and was unable to focus on my work. Once work was done, I ran home. Contrary to what I had feared, Rohan was at home. I yelled at him, 'Why didn't you answer my calls?'

He said that he was in deep trouble and that he had to leave because his parents were insisting that he immediately return to Holland. 'They don't know your worth,' he said. 'They yell at me. "Are you in love with an ali?" they ask. I need to make them understand things and change their mind. Then I'll marry you.'

I interrupted, 'Look Rohan! We don't live in Sri Lanka. We are both adults and we have the right to live our lives the way we want.' But he was determined to go. My heart told me that he would not return. When my sorrow turned into bitterness, I tried to jump out of the window. Rohan pulled me inside the room and slapped me. That was the first and last time that he hit me. He then punched the wall repeatedly. I stared at the blood-smeared wall and said, 'You may leave!'

44. The Gateway to Death

I silently looked at Rohan pack his bag and get dressed. Soon, he was ready to leave. He turned to me and said, 'I don't have money to buy a ticket.' I took some money from my purse and placed it on the table. He took the money and left.

I angrily stared at him until he walked out of the door. Then I looked down at the road through the window and saw him quickly walk away. I was unable to bear the pain so I ran after him. When I caught up with him, I grabbed his hand and begged him to come back home. I kept pleading with him until we reached the railway station. But he was determined to leave.

As Rohan waited for the train, I stood next to him silently crying. My heart soon grew cold. When the train arrived, Rohan said, 'I want to kiss you once before I leave.' As he tried to kiss me, I bit him hard on his cheek. He pushed me away but not before I had slapped him hard. He was stunned. The passengers at the station stared at us. 'Look, I'm a transwoman,' I said. I put my hands together in front of his face and clapped the way transwomen do in India. I then turned and left.

I bought some pills for a headache at a pharmacy. There were twenty tablets in a box. I went to two other stores and bought some more until I had sixty pills. I went back home and messaged my bank account number and the passwords for my bank and email accounts to my sister. She immediately called me. I wept and said, 'Rohan left me.' My sister asked me, 'Why did you send me your bank account details? Are you planning to end your own life?' I said no and then switched off the phone.

I sat down on the floor in the flat where Rohan and I had spent a month together. Rohan had left some of his clothes behind. I took his clothes and put them on my lap and howled. I cried till I had no tears left. After a while, I just stared at the floor not knowing what to do next.

On a piece of paper, I wrote, 'Amma, Anna and Akka, I love you but I love Rohan more.' I placed the paper on the dining table. The pills I had bought were waiting for me on the table. I took ten pills at a time and washed them down with water. I could feel the pills pass through my throat.

After I had taken thirty pills, I was nauseous and felt like vomiting. My body struggled to expel the pills. I swallowed the remaining thirty pills with great difficulty. I felt a weight on my body. My heart felt heavier. I slowly walked to the bed where Rohan and I had slept in each other's arms the previous night.

I muttered, 'I'll never find a fine lover like Rohan in this life.' The thought that he had left me for being a transwoman made me feel disgusted with my own life. As I lay on the bed and wept, my tongue grew stiff. My throat ached and felt dry. It felt like a thousand ants were crawling all over my legs. I thought they were the messengers of my wretched death.

As I began to slowly lose consciousness, the doorbell started to ring incessantly. I thought Rohan had changed his mind and had returned and so I staggered towards the door. My brother stood there. My sister had alerted him and asked him to check up on me.

When he entered the house, he saw the empty bottles lying on the dining table. He read my note. 'What the hell have you done?' he frantically asked. I wept, 'Rohan left me.' My brother retorted, 'Let that dog leave, we are here for you.' He carried me to his car and rushed towards the hospital. I vomited in the car.

When we reached the hospital, I was half-conscious. It was the same hospital I had been rushed to for taking thirty pills when I was sixteen. This time I had taken twice as many pills. The doctor on duty asked me, 'Why did you do this?' I solemnly replied, 'I'm unable to forget my lover. This world does not give me the right to live with him.' I lost consciousness at that moment.

45. Ceaseless Misfortune

When I regained consciousness and opened my eyes, it was 4 a.m. There was a telephone next to my bed. A little later, I received a call from Amma. I told her everything that had happened and dissolved into tears. Amma comforted me without getting anxious. 'Don't worry about anything,' she said. 'I gave birth to you, and I know how to make you happy.' A little while later, my sister called me. Her supportive words consoled me a little.

I called Priya Amma and told her everything. She scolded me for being so stupid. I called Kamini Chithi too. She was in Malaysia at the time. I remembered that she had already warned me that transwomen should never trust men and their loving words. I cried when I said to her, 'What you said came true.' She cried too and then consoled me. Although there was no one with whom I could share my joy, there was someone with whom I could share my misery.

My heart and body healed because of the love and support I received from my family and fellow transwomen. But I was unable to forget Rohan. I hoped that he would be anxious and distressed and rush to the hospital if he heard what I had done. I sent him a message on Facebook saying, 'I've been admitted to hospital because I tried to kill myself.' He did not respond even after reading my message. If I called him, he would disconnect my call.

I called his mother as I had her number. I said, 'I'm in the hospital because I tried to commit suicide after Rohan left me.' His mother said, 'It doesn't matter.' I asked her, 'Can I speak to Rohan?' She replied, 'We've found him a woman whose dowry is worth half a million rupees. Do you have that much money?' I was furious and ended the call. From that very instant, I erased Rohan from my heart.

I remained in the hospital for three days. On the fourth day, my family took me home. My brother asked one of his Tamil friends to stay in the flat that Rohan and I had taken on rent. I stayed at home and was not in the mood to do anything. Eventually, I received a letter that said I was dismissed from work for not turning up.

I suddenly went to a shop one day and got my navel pierced because I remembered that Rohan did not like women who pierced their navels. I was unemployed for the next three months. I spent this time talking to my imaginary friends and occasionally looking for jobs on the internet.

Soon, I encountered a new problem. I began to shed clumps of hair. I had alopecia when I was young. The same problem had returned. I did not pay attention to it because I still felt devastated. Finally, in February 2013 I got a job in a factory that made sweets. There was a young woman there who handled my documents. When I submitted my documents to her, I reluctantly said, 'I'm a transwoman. Please keep it to yourself and don't tell anyone.' That woman smiled at me kindly and said, 'Everyone has the right to work here.' When I received the contract, I immediately mailed it to the citizenship office.

I reluctantly went to work. I was always scared that my co-workers would discover that I am a transwoman. I was given the boring job of placing almonds on sweets that came out of a machine. I religiously placed almonds on sweets because my citizenship depended on this job.

My fellow workers were not welcoming. Many asked me, 'Why have you come here?' The first person to talk to me in a friendly manner was a Pakistani. Her name was Sonia. I noticed a Russian woman laughing at me. Sonia asked, 'Do you know why that woman is laughing at you?' I shook my head. 'She says that you look like a man because you're tall and you have facial hair.' When she said this I was broken.

Sonia could not tell that I was a transwoman. She simply thought that I was a masculine woman. I had lost five kilograms ever since I tried to kill myself. I really did look like a man in women's clothes because my face was gaunt and there was hair on certain parts of my face because I had not done my laser treatment for the past three months.

Sonia was thirty years old, unmarried and beautiful. She shared her lunch with me on days I forgot to bring mine. As we ate, she said, 'Something seems to be troubling you and it's making your face look pale. Take care of your health and wear good makeup. Be self-confident!' Her words encouraged me to start paying attention to my appearance again. Sonia suggested that I wear a wig to conceal the bald patches that had developed. I bought a long black wig and got my facial hair removed. I spent hours doing makeup.

A month passed. One day, as I was browsing the internet, I noticed something that made my heart sink. A mutual friend had shared Rohan's wedding pictures on Facebook. Rohan had gone to Sri Lanka and married a relative of his. He was grinning in the photographs. When I saw his grin, I was ashamed to think that I had tried to kill myself for him.

Rohan had often said that he would not abandon me. But eventually he had gone in search of a cis woman. As I wondered if he would have stayed with me had I been a cis woman who could have borne his child, I remembered his mother asking for a dowry of half a million rupees. That made me laugh bitterly.

I no longer wanted a life where I pursued men like a madwoman. I resolved to make men fall at my feet and beg for my love.

46. Rabeek

I went to work wearing a new look every day and became more popular at the factory. I walked upright and looked majestic, like a woman participating in a beauty contest. I was no longer humble and loving with my words. Instead, I grew insolent. My changed demeanour led to ample rewards.

The factory supervisor became smitten by my looks and made me an assistant supervisor. I got a small raise. I called myself Sana at the factory. My height and slim body drew men towards me. Many men asked me for my phone number and invited me to have drinks with them.

One of the workers was a Turkish man named Rabeek. He learnt a few Tamil words and tried to befriend me. He was about forty years old and was tall and muscular. He told me that he had made many Tamil friends at his previous workplace. He even sang a few lines from Tamil songs. He was a good singer. I gave him my phone number.

He called me on a Saturday morning and asked me to have lunch with him. I accepted his invitation because he was my colleague. I neither desired him nor did I have any other intentions. He said that he would pick me up in half an hour. I quickly showered and put on some makeup.

After Rabeek picked me up in his car, I asked him where we were going. He said, 'Let's go to my place first.' I knew that Rabeek lived alone. Although I was reluctant to go to his home, I was unable to refuse his loving invitation. He really was a sweet man. His words were somewhat mesmerising.

At his place, he asked me if I'd like a drink. I said that fruit juice was fine. He brought some alcohol for himself and some fruit juice for me in wine glasses. We sat close to each other and talked. There were hip-hop songs playing on the television.

Rabeek placed his hand on my shoulder as we spoke, but I reluctantly withdrew. Rabeek said, 'Don't be scared, Sana. I'm not a bad man.' But I said, 'No, I'm not ready for this.' He looked at me angrily and said, 'Are we going to talk all day?' He grew aggressive. However, despite my fear, I was also fond of him. I began to surrender to him.

As he showered my face with kisses, I asked him to give me some alcohol. When Rabeek went to get me a drink, I went to the toilet and lubricated my vagina. When I returned, he had poured me a generous amount of alcohol in a glass. After I finished my drink, I was ready to have sex.

The last time I had sex was with Rohan. After we separated, I had not used the rubber penis to widen the opening to my vagina. I felt that the opening had shrunk. Rabeek undressed me and then he took his own clothes off. His erect penis was very big. I felt distressed as I wondered how my vagina would accommodate his penis. I just wanted to escape.

Rabeek was quick to swing into action. He pressed his face against my vagina and caressed it. Then he inserted a finger inside and found that my vagina was narrow. He asked, 'Sana, are you a virgin?' I immediately said yes. He was astonished and asked again, 'You've never had sex?' I said I hadn't, because I thought he would let go of me if I said that. But Rabeek jumped with joy as though he had just won the lottery.

I pretended to be a virgin and asked him to be gentle with me. But he was excited by the thought of robbing a woman of her virginity and was rough instead. When he thrust his penis into my vagina, I felt a sharp pain erupt in my abdomen. I begged him to let go of me.

'I can't bear it,' I cried. 'It hurts.' But he just said, 'This is how it is the first time.' He continued to thrust. The inner walls of my vagina tore and began to bleed. He thought he had broken my hymen and continued to be rough. Once he was done, he happily embraced me.

'I need to go home now,' I said. He grinned and responded, 'You've given me this honour and now you want to go home?' But I insisted and so he reluctantly drove me home. 'I wanted your love and friendship, but you were despicable,' I said to him before I left his car.

I rushed to the bathroom and stood under the shower without removing my clothes. The water washed away the dry blood stains on my thighs. But what could I do about the blood oozing from my heart? Do these men know anything besides sexual aggression? I wondered.

Some men are ready to do anything to satisfy their frenzied desires. Their loving words and gestures disappear the moment their penises get aroused. I could not sleep that night. With whom could I share this act of cruelty? I summoned my imaginary friends and broke down while telling them what had happened.

47. The Women of Jaffna

When I was twenty-two, I met my first 'daughter', Esther, through Facebook. Esther was a transwoman living in Jaffna. I ritually adopted Esther as my daughter according to the practices of our community. Her friend Nirosha is still close to me. She has had her gender reassignment surgery. The two of them introduced me to some other transwomen from Jaffna. Through them I acquired new friendships.

Sri Lankan law acknowledges transwomen as women. But society is not ready to accept us. In an orthodox society where there is not even enough awareness about women's rights, how could anyone have any sympathy for transwomen? The transwomen of Jaffna feel trapped by their circumstances. But there are occasional rays of hope.

Esther told me that there were two transwomen in Jaffna who always dressed in female clothes. Their names were Sara and Mary. She gave me the former's number. I immediately called Sara. She had a sweet feminine voice. Sara told me that she was twenty-eight. She sounded calm and affectionate.

Sara was highly educated and fluent in English. She worked in an office and had saved money for her gender reassignment surgery. She told me that she would get the surgery done in India. However, the gender reassignment surgeries done in India were not good. They generally did not create an opening to have sex. I explained this to Sara. She asked me where she could go instead.

'My friend Rose went to Thailand to get her gender reassignment surgery done,' I told her. 'It'll be good if you get your surgery done at the same hospital. I'll try and accompany you to Thailand. I also need to enlarge my breasts.' When I said this, Sara became excited and said that she would go to Thailand with me.

When Sara spoke with joy, it was as if a bird was singing. Although I did not have any money to go to Thailand, I did not want to dampen her excitement. Later, she introduced me to her transwoman friend Maryamma. A hardworking person, Maryamma ran a business in the Sunnakam market and was financially comfortable.

Through her hard work, Maryamma had disproved the impression that all transwomen are destined to do sex work to survive. She described the lives of transwomen who live in Jaffna and the problems they face and introduced me to many transwomen from Jaffna. I wanted to work with them and help them as much as I could. Our individual advancement is related to the progress of the entire transwoman community.

48. A Lover from the Movies

I met an interesting person named Subbaiya through Facebook. He was a Sri Lankan Tamil who lived in Canada. He looked peculiar in his photographs, in which he was dressed in a suit with a cigar in his mouth. He introduced himself as a Tamil film producer and asked me for my number.

One day, Subbaiya called me and said, 'Miss, you're very beautiful. Would you like to act in my next movie?' I was not sure how far I could trust him. His Facebook profile was full of photographs of him standing with South Indian actors. 'If you wish you can become a cinema actress. Or we can continue to just remain friends,' he said.

Subbaiya often called me after that. The stories he told me about his life evoked my sympathy and compassion. He was about fifty years old but wasn't married. He said that he had spent his youth slogging in Canada to get his four sisters married. Although he had struggled in his youth, he was now busy producing movies and doing various other jobs.

Now Subbaiya lived a comfortable life but there was no one to take care of his palatial house because he was always rushing around for work. He asked me to come to Canada and stay with him. He said that I could assist him in producing movies.

I have been fascinated by Canada since I was young. But I still was not a German citizen, and I was still a man according to my Sri Lankan passport. Subbaiya thought that I was a woman. If I went to Canada with this passport, Subbaiya would discover that I'm a transwoman. I was reluctant to accept his invitation.

But Subbaiya did not accept my refusal. He asked me, 'Thanuja, will you be a good partner, someone who will be with me till the day I die?' His voice choked with emotion and I was moved. But I would no longer be deceived by men. I thought about it and finally decided that it might not be a mistake to say yes to this older man's request. It would be good to support each other. But what would happen if Subbaiya found out that I was a transwoman?

Subbaiya was more active than me on Facebook. It seemed like he was addicted to Facebook. He would look at the photographs I uploaded on Facebook and give his opinions on my appearance. He would say things like, 'You're truly beautiful, but your breasts are small. If you enlarge them, you'll look gorgeous.'

If transwomen in Germany want to enlarge their breasts, they first have to send an application to the medical insurance company. The company will pay for the surgery if their doctor approves the procedure. A doctor from the insurance company will examine the size of the breasts and only then give their approval for the surgery.

However, my breasts had emerged like small bags because of the hormones I had been taking. The medical insurance company refused to approve the surgery because as far as they were concerned, I had breasts. But that did not change my desire to enlarge them. The many men I had been with had made me feel insecure by commenting on my small breasts.

As the medical insurance company had rejected my request for breast enlargement, I would have to cover the entire cost of the surgery myself. In Germany, the procedure would cost over 5,000 euros. But in Thailand, the same procedure could be done for just 1,500 euros. So when Subbaiya asked me to enlarge my breasts, I laughed and said, 'If you pay for the surgery, I'll enlarge them.' He said that he was ready to pay. He had already been sending me gifts such as a sari and a cell phone from Canada.

Eight months after I joined the sweet factory, I was finally granted German citizenship. Now I was legally a woman. Once I received my citizenship papers, I quickly sent an application to the concerned department to change my gender. After it was approved, I could appear for job interviews as a woman. My dream of becoming a flight attendant was now within reach.

49. Thailand

Subbaiya did not break his promise and sent me the enormous sum of 3,000 euros. I immediately got to work. I spoke to Sara in Jaffna. She said that she was ready to go to Thailand. I emailed the hospital in Thailand and fixed appointments for both of our surgeries.

Sara reached Thailand two days before me. Her surgery was done by the time I landed in Bangkok. I went straight to the hotel where she was staying. The hotel was close to the hospital and was full of transwomen who had come for their surgeries. There were transwomen from every part of the world in that hotel.

Sara was lying in bed and welcomed me with a tired and happy expression. My friend Angel was also waiting for me there. She had come from Chennai just to meet me. She told me that she had already undergone her surgery there. Angel, as her name suggested, was truly an angel with wings. During the time we spent there, she flitted around taking care of us.

My appointment was at 8 a.m. the next day. Angel accompanied me to the hospital. The doctor examined me and said that he would implant 400 grams of silicone in my breasts because I was tall and had put on weight. Although I had thought of getting only 300 grams, I was happy with his suggestion. The doctor asked me to pay the cashier and wait.

Although I thought that I would be done soon, I was told that there were forty-one people ahead of me. The room was full of both transwomen and ciswomen who had come there to enlarge their breasts. Angel left me with them and went back to take care of Sara. The wait was long, and I was soon hungry.

My turn didn't come until 10 p.m. By then, I was feeling weak from hunger. When I lay down on the operating table, I fainted. I am not sure if it was from hunger or because of the drug they injected. While I was unconscious, they cut the skin under my arms and around my armpits and inserted silicone into my breasts.

When I regained consciousness, I deliriously began to chant the Mahishasura Mardini Stotra. I heard the doctor's voice faintly calling out to me. I put my palms together and thanked him as I kept chanting. It felt as if I had rocks in my breasts and I struggled to breathe. I was transferred to another room. Those who had undergone their surgeries were lying in that room.

One of the people recovering there was a transwoman from the Philippines who had undergone gender reassignment surgery. When she regained consciousness, she began moaning in pain. She was muttering in English, 'The pain is too much. Please turn me back into a man.' I wanted to go close to her and comfort her, but I couldn't stand.

I was unable to sleep at all that night in the midst of these transwomen who were crying and moaning. By the next morning, the pain in my breasts had slightly receded. Angel came to take me back to the hotel. Sara was still lying in bed, unable to walk. I lay close to her and soon fell asleep.

When I woke up, it was evening. The pain in my breasts had largely subsided. I eagerly looked at my breasts in the mirror. They had swelled but they still looked beautiful. I called Priya Amma and told her about my surgery. She said that 400 grams of silicone was too much. She then suggested that I get my nose and jawline surgically modified to look more like a woman.

I took her advice and went back to the doctor. The doctor examined my face and said, 'God has given you a beautiful face. I can change your face with surgery, but it will not look natural. There will be many side effects. Over time, you may even begin to look ugly. You already have a woman's face, don't change it.'

I stayed in Thailand for two weeks. Angel and I roamed around Bangkok and sampled a variety of Thai dishes. We went shopping and bought a lot of clothes and also went to discos to dance. After a fortnight, I said my goodbyes to Angel and Sara and returned to Germany.

Amma was amazed to see my swollen breasts. She muttered in dissatisfaction, 'They are too large.' But I loved my new breasts. I was happy that I had become a complete woman. However, Subbaiya ruined my happiness by frequently calling and asking me to come to Canada.

I sensed that he suspected that I was trying to get rid of him after taking his money. It was never my intention to deceive him. I truly wished to go to Canada. No one in Canada knew my past. I thought I could identify as a complete woman and start a new life there.

I was still classified as a man in my new German passport. I was conflicted because I did not know how to tell Subbaiya this. By then Subbaiya had sent me money for the flight ticket. I hoped to somehow settle this issue and got ready to go to Canada. My search for a new life made me leave Germany. Amma reluctantly agreed to let me go.

50. Canada

I flew from Düsseldorf to Vancouver via London. At the airport, I was granted a six-month visa. Subbaiya had told me that he would be waiting for me at the airport. I looked for him at the airport but did not see him anywhere. When I called him, his phone was switched off.

After two hours, he called me back and said, 'I'm just leaving home now.' I waited for another hour before he arrived. I thought he resembled the veteran actor S.V. Ranga Rao with his large curly moustache and the cap on his head. He hugged me and greeted me in English. He was taller than me and seemed three times my size.

'I didn't know when your flight would land,' he said with a crooked smile. He seemed neither educated nor rational. I could not understand how a man like him could be a businessman. He wheeled my trolley towards the parking lot but he had forgotten where he parked his car. It took a while before he finally found his car.

On the way to his home he kept telling me how great Canada was. Subbaiya's house was a little distance from Vancouver in a place called Delta. It was not very cold at the time. The weather seemed similar to Germany. Although Subbaiya's house was not the palace that he had said it was, it was certainly big. He had rented the ground floor to a Jamaican woman and her daughter while he lived on the top floor.

I had dinner with Subbaiya and then retired to the room he had prepared for me with many thoughts running through my mind. I did not find Subbaiya attractive at all. The next morning, I stood on the balcony drinking tea and admiring the natural beauty around me. Many Indians lived in the neighbourhood. I saw many turbaned Sikhs pass by.

By the afternoon, the Jamaican woman who lived downstairs and I had become friends. Her name was Alice and she was around sixteen years old. We began talking about the young Sikh men in the area. She said she knew some of them. She had downloaded an application called Danko on her phone and used it to find her male friends.

Alice asked me if I was going to marry Subbaiya. 'That's what he told us,' she revealed. I denied that I was there to marry him. 'I'm just his friend,' I said. 'That's what I thought,' Alice said, smiling. 'You're a young woman. It wouldn't be right to marry an older man like him.' The answer to my confused thoughts lay in her smile.

When Subbaiya took me out that afternoon, he bought me a SIM card for my phone. I downloaded the application that Alice had told me about and connected with several men in a matter of minutes. They all asked me for my phone number. I gave my number to a few Sikh men because I liked them the most. They called me and occasionally chatted with me.

I soon discovered that Subbaiya was not a businessman. He had lied that he was a film producer just to bring me to Canada. He was actually a long-distance truck driver. He had also claimed to be younger than he actually was. In reality, he was nearing sixty. But what was the point of fighting with him? I too had concealed a major truth about myself.

When Subbaiya left on a driving shift, he would only return two weeks later. As I did not wish to be alone for so long, he introduced me to Vijaya, a woman who ran a provision store that sold Sri Lankan and Indian products in Vancouver. Subbaiya suggested that I spend my time assisting her with the shop.

I was lonely after he left. Time went by slowly as I cooked, ate, slept and browsed the internet. I was soon bored of going to Vijaya's shop. That was when my Danko friend Karan asked me to meet him at his home. I accepted his invitation. He was a Sikh who lived alone in a large house.

Karan told me that he was the head of a sanitation company. He seemed to live a comfortable life and served me an elaborate meal. After lunch, we drank some alcohol and listened to Punjabi songs. Soon, it was time for sex. Karan was smitten by my naked body. He kept asking me, 'How are your breasts so beautiful?'

After we had sex, he confessed that he had a wife and two children. I did not create a fuss because I had already heard many such confessions. I only needed someone to ease my loneliness and give me sexual pleasure. Besides, he was rich. We kept in touch. Karan gave me a lot of money for my expenses. He was deeply in love with me. But I was determined never to be sincere with a man again. I had suffered enough betrayals for being sincere.

I soon met another young Sikh man named Ronnie through Danko. Ronnie was a truck driver as well. He was twenty-five, handsome and single. He took me to a disco. I found Ronnie affectionate and always smiling. We drank and made merry all night and then got into his car at about 4 a.m.

I saw some drunken men stumbling on the road. I thought people drank more in Canada than they did in Europe. They also fought more in public. However, Ronnie and I did not fight—we made love in the car. We kissed and then Ronnie bit my breasts in a fit of desire. My breasts turned red and sore. He left marks on my neck as well. When I said that I had to get back home, he drove me home right away.

51. The Sensational Hero

I stopped assisting Vijaya because I spent most of my time with Ronnie and Karan. Subbaiya called and shouted, 'Why haven't you been going to the shop?' I began to argue and our argument escalated. He was right to suspect that I would abandon him. Subbaiya then asked me to bear him a child. 'Alright,' I said. 'Let's talk when you're back.'

I started going to Vijaya's shop again to pacify Subbaiya. I helped her at the store despite soon being tired of standing among sacks of chilli powder and *appalam* packets. I endured it as I waited for Subbaiya to return. My boredom was eased when a lively and attractive young Tamil man visited the store. I thought I had seen him somewhere. It did not take me long to recognise him. He had acted in a short movie on YouTube. I told him that he acted well. He got excited when I said this and told me that his name was Naren and that he acted in Canadian Tamil movies. He lived in Toronto and was visiting Vancouver to attend a film festival. He forgot what he wanted to buy at the shop once we began talking about cinema.

We connected on Facebook and became friends. Naren soon began to comment on the pictures I had uploaded on Facebook. I had no reason to dislike him. But when I understood from his Facebook posts that he was married, I did not hope for anything more. On Karthigai Deepam, I uploaded a picture of myself with the lamps I had lit in Subbaiya's house. Naren immediately commented, 'I didn't know you were as beautiful as a lamp.' We chatted for a while and even exchanged numbers.

From then, Naren began calling me incessantly. He was kind and funny and would imitate Tamil actors to make me laugh. Talking to him made me happy. I never felt that I was talking to a stranger. When I finally asked about his wife, he began to sob like a child. 'I was in love with my wife when I got married to her,' Naren cried. 'But after we got married, we were not happy. We spent our days fighting. My wife soon left me. Now we are waiting to get divorced. My life has been destroyed.' He wept and made a scene. I patiently and lovingly consoled him almost like a nanny.

Even as my friendship with Naren grew, I kept in touch with the Sikh men. Intoxicated by love, Karan would promise to make me his second wife. Ronnie was different. He was sincere and never tried to sweet-talk me into things and he was never oversmart. He was the first man who never inflicted any physical pain on me. He understood my body when we had sex.

I spent a day with Ronnie and returned home late at night. I noticed that Naren had called me many times. When I called him back, he was drunk and in a terrible frenzy. 'Why didn't you receive my calls?' he yelled. I told him that I was with my lover Ronnie. Naren asked, 'Is Ronnie Tamil?' I said that he wasn't. Naren began to say, 'It's not right to be with men from other communities, Thanuja. They'll deceive you—' I cut him off and yelled, 'Naren, Tamil men have cheated me as well! I know that the Tamil culture and morality they talk of is deceptive.' I wished him a good night and ended the call.

The next morning, Naren began to cross-examine me over a Skype call. He did not let me do any work and kept talking. After two days of constant talking, he said, 'I'm in love with you, Thanuja.' I told him that I didn't love him. 'I just like you,' I said. 'Let's be friends and not go beyond that.'

Naren began to recite dramatic lines like 'Thanuja, only you can end my pain'. He told me that he would marry me. 'I'm not like any ordinary Tamil man,' he insisted. 'I respect you and I'll treat you as an equal. I'll treat you like an angel.' I made fun of him in response. 'O actor!' I mocked. 'Stop with your movie lines!'

However, I was lost in thought that night. What would become of my future? After Rohan left me, several men had used me for their sexual pleasure. I did not think I could live with Subbaiya. In fact, when I looked through Subbaiya's computer, I discovered that he had been watching gay porn. That probably explained why he was still unmarried and had never made sexual advances towards me.

A part of me still wished to be an ordinary married woman who had her own family. That would be good for my future. Once I had thought about this, I decided to accept Naren's love. I informed him of my consent the next day. Naren became very emotional and wept with joy. I called Ronnie and Karan the next day and told them, 'I'm in love with someone else. We can no longer be friends.' They tried to dissuade me but I refused to relent. I let the spark of love that Naren lit engulf me.

I met Naren at a restaurant that evening. He made me laugh so much that I could not eat properly. I was possessed by his affectionate words and loving gestures. If someone possesses my heart, I become an ardent lover like the Tamil Vaishnava Bhakti poet Andal Nachiyar. This is what happened. I realised that Naren was a lovely man and did not have the heart to let go of him that night. So, I accompanied him to the hotel where he was staying.

When I had sex with Naren, I felt his absolute love. There is no better place than the bed for a woman to feel that kind of thing. Naren was not with me merely for his sexual pleasure. He truly loved me. Rather than his body, I became a slave to the joy his heart gave me. No man I had known till then had given me so much hope.

Naren told me that his divorce would come through in a few months and then we would get married as soon as possible. He spent three joyous days with me before returning to Toronto. He said that he would soon take me to Toronto with him. I thought I should no longer conceal the fact that I am a transwoman,

Naren called me once he reached Toronto. I tried to tell him the truth, but I fumbled for words. I hesitatingly began, 'I need to tell you something, Naren…' My long preamble scared him. He thought that I was about to end our relationship and began sobbing. I managed to overcome my hesitation and blurted, 'I can never have a child.' He asked me why through his sobs. 'I wasn't born a woman,' I said. When I put it this way, most men I had been with would be confused. The same thing happened with Naren. 'I don't understand,' he sobbed. I asked him, 'Have you heard of transwomen? I'm one of them.' He suddenly became annoyed. 'You're just making something up to break up with me,' he said.

I told him that I really was a transwoman. 'You asked me about the scars under my armpits, right?' I asked. 'Well, they are from the surgery I had to get silicone breasts.' I told him the truth of my life. Naren was silent until I had told him everything. Then he burst into more tears. He was shattered by my story.

Finally, he said that he had no problem with me being a transwoman but asked me not to tell anyone else. 'I also want to conceal the truth as far as possible,' I said. Even after I told him the truth, Naren's love for me did not diminish in the least. He said that he would not tell his parents the truth and still marry me.

After that I never spoke to him about my identity as a transwoman. I devoted myself to him. In fact, I thought I would be deliberately betraying Naren if I continued to live with Subbaiya. Naren did not know the truth about my relationship with Subbaiya because I had told him that he was my uncle.

I waited restlessly for Subbaiya to return from his latest work trip. When he finally came back home, I gently told him, 'I'm in love with a Tamil man from Toronto. I want you to let me leave.' When he heard this, Subbaiya went into a frenzy. He said that he would be the one to marry me. He claimed that he had already told the entire city about it.

I said very calmly, 'That'll never happen. Besides, I think you're gay. The right thing for you to do would be to look for a partner. We'll not be compatible.' Subbaiya retorted, 'If you don't like being here, go back to Germany! I'll buy you the ticket.' When I agreed, he asked me to immediately buy a ticket online for the first plane flying out the next day.

There was a morning flight from Vancouver to Montreal. I would have to catch another flight from there to Germany. I paid for the ticket with Subbaiya's credit card. I called Naren and said, 'My uncle knows about our relationship. He's forcing me to go back to Germany tomorrow morning.' We carefully made our plans. Naren sent me a plane ticket from Montreal to Toronto that very night.

Subbaiya took me to the airport the next morning and wheeled my suitcase to the entrance. I embraced him and said goodbye. He forced me to take 300 dollars in cash. 'You're a loving man,' I began. 'But—' He cut me off by saying, 'Let's not talk.' He turned and quickly walked away. When I checked in for the flight, I told the person at the counter that I was flying only as far as Montreal.

52. The Man of My Dreams

It took six hours to fly from Vancouver to Montreal. During the flight, I could not think of anything but

Naren. I did not even think of my own family. After I landed in Montreal, I switched to the flight to Toronto. It took ninety minutes to reach Toronto from Montreal.

Naren was waiting for me at the airport. He gave me a long hug with tears in his eyes. My heart softened and I began to float even as I was standing. I was overwhelmed by Naren's love. The satisfaction of having found the man of my dreams filled my soul.

It was December and I could not bear the Toronto winter. This winter was more severe than any of the winters I had experienced in my life. Naren lived in Scarborough. We drove to a large and beautiful house where he had lived with his wife until some months ago. I could see traces of his married life inside the house. The photographs of his wedding were still hanging on the wall. They bothered me.

I cooked dinner that night. 'You're the first woman to cook in this house,' Naren said. He told me that his wife did not know how to cook. I felt that there was a ray of hope in my life. After that first day, I spent every moment immersed in his love.

New Year's Day arrived. I made resolutions for 2014 because now I had found a true lover. I would not drink alcohol nor visit discos and I would not be with other men. I wanted to visit a temple to celebrate the New Year. Naren took me to the Ganesh temple in Toronto.

Some of his friends were waiting at the temple. I was overjoyed when he held my hand and introduced me as his partner. His refined friends did not pester me with questions. We entered the temple and prayed. Naren asked me to close my eyes. After I did so, he put some kumkum in the parting of my hair. I was moved.

'As far as our hearts are concerned, we are husband and wife with God as our witness.' When Naren said this, I touched his feet like a good wife would. My dream was to live the life of a complete woman in Tamil society bearing all the auspicious signs of a wife. I fulfilled this dream through Naren. The kumkum cooled my forehead.

We truly lived as husband and wife until I received some news from my brother that interrupted our joy. He told me that I had received permission to officially change my gender and name but I would have to go to the court in Cologne to make the changes to my documents. This was very important to me.

When I told Naren that I would have to go to Germany to complete all the legal formalities, he was disappointed. He feared that I would forget him if I went to Germany. After I made him understand my situation, he half-heartedly agreed to let me go but asked me to visit his parents before leaving.

His parents lived in Mississauga. When we went to their apartment, his mother was alone at home. She was about sixty. She did not welcome me or even say anything until she looked at my hair and asked, 'Is that a wig?' I was taken aback. Men never suspected that I wore wigs. I regained my composure and said, 'This is my natural hair.'

Although Naren's mother made me a nice cup of milky tea, she did not talk much. However, at the Ganesh temple in Toronto I had prayed that she should not ask me anything. We did not tell her that we already lived together. We made sure we did not disappoint her and left after a while.

I said goodbye to Naren with the hope that we would meet again. He wept and lamented my departure. I comforted him before leaving for the airport. When the plane took off, I burst into tears. I wept all the way to Germany.

53. The Days in Paris

Amma was overjoyed when I returned home. My brother was affectionate too, but Appa was just drunk as usual. He had become an alcoholic. I spent most of my time at home paying stamp fees to change my documents and mailing my certificates. I chatted with Naren day and night on Skype. He writhed like a worm unable to bear our separation. He told me that on his bed he had spread the sari that I had worn to the temple on New Year's Day.

Changing my documents was a long-drawn process. The officials asked for many certificates but objected to every certificate that I sent them. I was still tirelessly arguing with them in February, when Naren decided to give me a pleasant surprise for Valentine's Day. He took a week off from work and came to Paris without telling me.

He called me and said, 'I'm waiting for you in Paris.' I was truly astonished. I had not expected Naren to travel so far just to see me. He told me that he was staying with a cousin there. I took the next train to Paris. I was waiting at the station when Naren and his boisterous friends arrived. I playfully hid behind a pillar and observed them. He looked for me everywhere and began to cry when he could not find me. That was when I ran and embraced him.

We drove to Naren's cousin's house. The cousin was at work. Naren's friends left us alone. We compensated for a month's separation and our lovemaking was moving and frenzied. We were both ecstatic. Then, I took a bath and cooked dinner.

While we were eating, Naren's cousin returned home from work and joined us. He complimented my cooking. Naren had told me that he was separated from his wife and lived alone. I thought Naren's cousin had a gentle nature. He was very polite to me.

That evening, Naren and I stepped out holding hands. We furiously kissed each other below the Eiffel Tower. Above our heads, the illuminated tower glowed. There were many people selling roses on the streets. Naren bought roses from each of the sellers we met and offered them to me. We went to La Chappelle, a place that was full of Tamil shops.

Those days in Paris were sweet, but soon Naren had to return to Canada. His cousin and I saw him off at the airport. Naren was unable to let go of me and kept crying. I was crying too. The moment Naren left, his cousin asked me, 'Why do you love him?' I was surprised. 'Who wouldn't like such a loving man?' I asked. The cousin thought for a while and then said, 'He's a liar! When he is not lying, he only opens his mouth when he has to drink. He cannot live without alcohol. That is how he ruined the life of that woman in Canada and now he's going to ruin yours ...'

I had heard someone else complain about Naren earlier. When I was in Canada, his friend had told me the same thing. He had also added that Naren's emotions were exaggerated because he had a habit of smoking weed. What his friend said may have been true because of the way Naren spoke. But Naren had never smoked weed in my presence.

I firmly said to Naren's cousin, 'Whatever it may be ... I'm in love with Naren. I'll live with him no matter what happens. My love will slowly change him.' Naren's cousin appreciated my self-confidence. He saw me off at the railway station.

54. At My Mother-in-Law's

Naren and I resumed our love life over the phone. He would drink every night with his friends and then call me. It would be early morning in Germany when he called. I would wake up early and wait for his call. He would first apologise for drinking before saying anything else. I could not understand half of what he said because he would slur.

Soon, I found out that the house where he and I had stayed in Canada belonged to his wife. Naren was living with his parents now that his wife had claimed ownership of her house. He spent his days drinking and harassing his parents. I could not understand why he continued to drink and destroy himself even when a woman like me had entered his life. Whenever I asked him not to drink, he would sob and swear that he would stop drinking.

Eventually, Naren was arrested for drunk driving and his driving licence was confiscated. He drank more to get over that incident. He once fought with another Tamil man at a bar and assaulted him. Charges were pressed and he had to appear in court. He soon lost his job for not showing up at work. Naren spent all day drinking and when he called me at night he would fight with me.

My life gradually became hell again. I would go to bed crying and wake up feeling anxious. When Naren was sober, he would call up and apologise for fighting with me. I would immediately forgive him like Jesus Christ. But he would again start drinking that night. 'I drink only because I'm unable to bear our separation,' he claimed. 'I'll not drink like this if you're with me.' When he said this, I thought I should try and take care of him.

I still had not been able to change my name and gender in my documents, but I could still travel to Canada. I asked Naren, 'If I visit you, where will I stay?' He immediately said that there was no problem as he had already spoken to his mother. 'You can stay with me in my parents' house,' he said. As I was reluctant to believe him, Naren made me talk to his mother. She confirmed that I could stay with them. The thought of meeting Naren again made my anger dissolve like dew in summer. I bought my ticket and some gifts for Naren's family and flew to Toronto with love brimming in my heart.

Naren was waiting for me at the airport with a bouquet of roses. When he saw me, he hugged and kissed me. The stench of alcohol overpowered the fragrance of the roses. He said that he drank because he was happy that I was coming. We travelled in his friend's car because Naren was no longer permitted to drive.

I reluctantly stepped into Naren's parents' house. His mother welcomed me with only her eyes. I went to Naren's room, kept my things on his bed and sat down. I was scared to leave the room. Naren forced me to come to the living room. Naren's mother served tea. I thanked her, had my tea and then took our empty cups to the kitchen to wash them.

Naren's mother yelled at him, 'Ask her not to do anything in the kitchen.' It was a miracle that my anxious hands did not drop the cups and break them. I left the cups in the kitchen and modestly sat down in front of his mother. She looked at me and asked, 'Why did you trust him and come here?' I was shocked and did not know what to say.

After Naren left the room, I was trapped with his mother. She told me that she disapproved of the lipstick I wore and then again looked at my hair. I was scared that she would suddenly spring to her feet and grab hold of my wig. She had dyed her hair and was wearing lipstick herself, but she taunted and hurt me.

I went to Naren's room and cried while staring at the wall. How was I going to spend time in this house? Naren consoled me and fought with his mother. She immediately came and said, 'I'll never say anything to you again. You may do as you please.' Then she turned and left.

In a short while, Naren's father returned from work. He greeted me and then immediately asked, 'Why did you trust him and come all the way to Canada?' I was silenced as I wondered if this was the family question. Naren's father kept cross-examining me. I muttered my answers. Naren's parents spoke to each other in sign language like characters in a play. They raised their voices at the most unexpected moments and suddenly asked questions. I had become a new character in their play.

That night, Naren had sex with me without any concern for my feelings. I had a habit of cleaning my vagina after sex, but Naren stopped me because he thought his parents would get suspicious if I went to the bathroom in the middle of the night. I lay hugging Naren feeling very confused.

The next morning, after my bath I went to the kitchen and prayed that I do not quarrel with Naren's mother. I smeared some sacred ash on my forehead and started cleaning the house. Naren's mother looked at me with a broomstick in her hand and said, 'No one else has cleaned this house.' Later, she and I cooked together. That was when she opened her heart to me.

Naren's mother told me that she was very worried that the Tamils in Canada led immoral lives. She slandered the lives of domestic Tamil women living in foreign countries. Later, she told me that she did not like that I had left my hair undone. She asked me to braid my hair. I obeyed her like a good daughter-in-law.

Naren's mother would be affectionate one moment and angry the next. I never understood her moods. Naren's father did not talk much to me. He rarely showed any emotions. Another problem I faced living there was that I had to wear my wig all the time. I could remove it only when I had a bath. However, my alopecia was slowly healing and the bald spots were growing new hair.

55. Beyond Sorrow

A few days after I moved into Naren's family home, he got a new job. I began to wake up at 5 a.m. and make tea for him. Then I would iron his clothes and keep them ready for him by the time he finished bathing. Finally I would make sandwiches and pack them in his lunch box before seeing him off as he left for work. I would then sleep for a couple of hours. Getting up again at 8 a.m., I would have a shower and finish all my household chores while fervently praying that I did not fight with Naren's mother that day.

She would only wake up at 10 a.m. We would cook and do the laundry together and then sit down to watch television. She had accepted me as her companion but there were no signs of her accepting me as her daughter-in-law. Naren's father was happy to see us getting along. He sometimes chatted with me too. I began to believe that he was truly fond of me.

Once Naren got back from work, we would sit in our room and talk for some time. Then we would go and have coffee at Tim Hortons, a local café chain.

The coffee there was terrible. It was like drinking hot water but the Canadians believe that is what coffee is. I would reluctantly drink it because it was important for me to spend time with Naren outside.

I gradually began to like this life. I had turned into a domestic Tamil woman with a husband, parents-in-law and responsibilities. I forgot that I was a transwoman. Naren's mother would not let me step out alone and I almost lived the life of a slave. But I liked this life. Since my childhood, my dream was to live like an ordinary Tamil woman. I believed that I had finally fulfilled this dream. But luck was never on my side.

There were two young Tamil men living in the same apartment complex. Naren would sometimes visit them, and they would drink together. When I first started to live with him and his parents, Naren did not visit these friends of his often. But soon, Naren began spending most of his evenings there. He gradually stopped giving me attention.

Naren's mother told me that those young men were weed addicts. She would order me to call Naren and force him to come back if he was at their place. If I hesitated, she would fight with me. But if I called him, Naren would fight with me. Naren's drinking habit grew worse. He would roam around after work and come back home looking sloshed.

Even if he was absolutely drunk, he never forgot to have sex with me. I developed a urinary tract infection because I did not clean myself after sex. I always carried antibiotics with me, and I felt fine after having one of them. But the pain lasted for three days. I endured pain in my body and heart only because of my undying love for Naren.

Naren's mother was angry about her inability to control Naren's alcoholism and began directing her anger towards me. I was twice as angry with Naren. On a day off, Naren tried to appease me by saying he'd take me out to dinner. Going out was a rare opportunity, so I happily dressed up. I liked looking attractive when I dressed up, but I ended up looking modest keeping in mind my mother-in-law's gaze.

Naren took me to a nearby bar. This did not make me happy. But I did not wish to miss even a moment with Naren. Little did I know that I would be in trouble. Men on the street and in the bar stared at me because I was tall and had an attractive figure. I was not sure if the attention I received made me happy or sad. I was anxious because instead of looking at me Naren was staring at the men who were staring at me. He chugged his drinks. When he was drunk, he decided to thrash those would-be Romeos.

I tried to get him out of the bar. We left and went to an Indian restaurant. There Naren began to quarrel with a waiter who did not attend to us. He did not listen to me and swore at the waiter. The waiter was arguing with Naren when Naren took something from the table and struck the waiter. The other waiters rushed to grab Naren and called the police. I was consumed by humiliation. Unable to bear it, I left the place before the police arrived.

I walked back home. Naren's mother was sitting in the drawing room when I entered. She was not happy to see me return alone. I did not tell her what happened, instead saying that Naren had gone somewhere with his friends. I went to my room and lay there crying.

I tried to call Naren several times, but his phone was dead. I was awake all night with tears in my eyes. Naren returned at 4 a.m. He was still drunk. 'What happened?' I asked. He did not reply and just fell asleep the moment he lay down.

56. The Wedding Sari

I spent my days fighting and reconciling with Naren. His parents grew closer to me and gave their blessings for Naren and me to get married. Once, the two of them went shopping and bought me a silk sari for the wedding. I trembled with joy and touched their feet. Naren's father smiled and said, 'Get married soon. Live in your own house after you get married. My wife and I wish to live in peace.'

When Naren returned in the evening, he was thrilled when I showed him the wedding sari. I told him we would soon be married and asked him to promise that he would not drink again. Naren qualified the promise and said, 'I won't drink a lot.' But even as we began to plan for the wedding, there came a letter from the police addressed to Naren.

His mother read the letter with the little English that she knew, asked me a few questions and understood what had happened. The letter charged Naren with assaulting a waiter in a restaurant. The police had registered a case against Naren. I called Naren and informed him when he was at work. He casually said, 'Let's talk in the evening.'

I could not blame his mother for being angry with me because I was with him on the evening the incident took place. She scolded him for as long as she could and then began crying. I tried to console her. She caressed my cheek and told me, 'You're a good child, you've been raised well. Don't marry this scoundrel!' I began to cry too.

I had to return to Germany because if I did not change my name and gender in my documents before registering my upcoming marriage, there would be legal complications. More importantly, Naren's parents would discover that I am a transwoman. Early the next morning, I helped Naren get ready and then embraced and kissed him. I saw him off to work with a happy face. Once he left, my face changed. I wept and wept. I felt that I could not be without him.

His parents took me to the airport. I cried on the way. They consoled me by saying, 'You will soon return and get married to him. Don't worry.' They had accepted me as their daughter-in-law. I was happy yet utterly heartbroken like one of those sunny days when it rains. My imaginary friends told me, 'You're never going to see Naren again.'

Naren called me before my flight. I sobbed, 'I may never see you again.' He promised that he would never let go of me. I flew from Toronto to Dublin. I had to catch a connecting flight from Dublin and there was an hour between flights. I called Naren, who began to cry. Listening to him cry made me cry as well.

We took turns crying and I did not realise that the plane I had to catch had left. I had to wait for another twelve hours in Dublin before taking the next flight to Germany.

57. Legally a Woman

There were more than ten transwomen waiting at the high court in Cologne on the day of my hearing to have my gender and name officially changed. I waited for half an hour before I was asked to enter the interview room. The judge asked me a few questions and then declared, 'From today your name is Thanuja and you're legally a woman.' He looked at me. I put my palms together and bowed.

The judge smiled and stamped the document with a seal and gave it to me. I received the document feeling ecstatic and left the room with tears running down my cheeks. My struggle had come to an end. From today, I would no longer have to tell anyone that I'm a transwoman. I had become a woman!

I changed my name and gender in all my documents including my passport and school certificates. The German government issued me a new birth certificate now that I was a German citizen. I had a brief quarrel with the office that issued birth certificates and made them change my gender on my birth certificate to female. I visited the Aachen registration office and signed a note of confidentiality that forbids the office from revealing my former name and gender to anyone.

Naren and I fought incessantly once I returned from Canada. There was a time when I would eagerly wait for his call but now his calls scared me. If that was not enough, Naren's mother would call me with a series of complaints against Naren. His drunken fights on the road had now started at home.

Amma was sad to see me fight with Naren and cry every day. She asked me, 'Do you deserve such an accursed life? Don't suffer all your life by marrying a drunk like I did.' But I was unable to accept what she said. I had deliberately trapped myself in this situation.

All transwomen go through this at least once in their life. We cannot easily let go of the men we deeply love. It is because they acknowledge us as women. We are ready to lose and sacrifice anything for a lover who acknowledges us. Even if he oppresses us, we struggle to let go of him. I believed that I would never find another man in my life who loves me with all his heart like Naren did. The very thought made me surrender to him.

Naren wanted to go to India and act in Tamil movies. When one of his friends visited Chennai for three months, he asked him to look for opportunities. Naren quit his job and began preparing to move to India. I did not object to his plans but I asked him to marry me before going to India.

However, Naren's love for cinema was greater than his love for me. He refused to listen to my entreaties and left. I had sacrificed so much to make him happy. But Naren was not ready to sacrifice anything for me. He bullied me in the name of love. I had mistaken his unfair dominance for undying love and concern.

58. The Oldest Profession

Priya Amma called me when she learnt that I was back from Canada. She had moved to Hamburg in Germany because there were legal prohibitions against sex work in Switzerland. She lived with a Malaysian transwoman named Iyer Savitri who was also a sex worker.

I asked Priya, 'How long will you run from country to country doing sex work on the sly?' She responded with a question, 'I'm not educated like you. Who will give me a job?' I did not have an immediate response and I'm sure you, the reader, do not have one either.

There was some misunderstanding between her and Iyer Savitri. Priya wanted to work on her own. She asked me to look for an apartment in Cologne from where she could work independently. I searched online until I was exhausted and eventually found a room on rent that would match her requirements.

Priya Amma came to Cologne the next day. I went to meet her there and we took a look at the room. The room was in a crowded part of Cologne. The owner was waiting for us there. We paid a week's rent and took the keys. The room was neat with a cot and furniture and a modern-looking bathroom.

I looked online for clients for Priya Amma by uploading her photograph and phone number. Not even five minutes had passed when her phone began to ceaselessly ring. Priya's German was not fluent so I negotiated with them. The price would be 150 euros. I would leave the room and walk down the street when we were expecting a client. Priya would call me after the client had left.

It was comforting to be with Priya Amma rather than being trapped in my room in Aachen crying and lamenting at the thought of Naren. Priya Amma's business started to go well. Naren often called me from India and pestered me for money. When I told him I did not have any, he would call me names.

I cried and cried unable to bear his harsh words. My hatred for him emerged from my tears. When I had no tears left, my heart began to withdraw from him. Priya Amma took care of me during my misery. She consoled me by saying, 'No one but transwomen can support another transwoman! Don't respect anyone who tortures you. Erase him from your heart! You need to create your own happiness.'

She told me to become a sex worker like her. Although I was reluctant to do sex work, I was conflicted when I saw how much money Priya Amma made. My hatred for Naren only added to my conflict. Finally, I too joined the oldest profession in the world.

One of Priya Amma's clients became my first client. When he visited Priya, she told him that her beautiful younger sister was visiting. He was asked to pay 150 euros for half an hour with me. When the client agreed, Priya called me to the room.

When I entered, I saw a tall white man standing behind Priya feeling up her buttocks. When he saw me, he let go of Priya and pounced on me. He made me lie down and kissed me. Priya gave me some lubrication which I smeared in my vagina. The white man had sex with me and ejaculated in a minute.

This truly was an easy way of forgetting Naren. The subtleties and transformations of human hearts are a mystery. When someone else touched my body, Naren receded from my heart. From that very moment, I stopped thinking about marriage, family life and Tamil culture. I could only think of making money. I worked the entire week and saved over a 1,000 euros even after spending a lot. Priya Amma and I divided the rent between us.

Although Naren's memory had grown faint, I could not forget him entirely. Whenever he called me, my accursed heart would struggle like a wingless dragonfly. If he asked me for money, I sent him the money I earned. He spent my money drinking and celebrating with his friends in Chennai.

59. Iyer Savitri

Priya Amma's former roommate Iyer Savitri asked for Priya's help as she was unable to manage on her own. Although Priya and Iyer had disagreements, Priya still welcomed her as she firmly believed that transwomen have to help each other. There is no one else to help us.

Iyer joined us in Cologne. She had undergone several surgeries on her face and body. In her attempt to look beautiful and feminine, she had begun to look strange. As we were eating, I asked her, 'Why do they call you Iyer?' She told me that she had gone to India when she was still a man. There, she learnt Vedic chants and then began to work as a priest at a temple in Malaysia. But she could no longer work at temples when she began to identify as a transwoman. Her family could not accept her transformation. Eventually, she became a sex worker.

The three of us worked together. We negotiated with the police and the rogues and abused our bodies to earn money. Priya Amma told me to forget Naren, who would still keep calling. She tried to teach me her own life's lesson, because she too had a man she loved with all her heart, but he exploited her. 'He didn't care that I made money by abusing my own body,' she told me. 'He used my money to have affairs with other women. Finally, he died in an accident because I cursed him. We mustn't be blinded by our lovers' love and kindness. We must always keep our eyes open.'

Despite what Priya Amma said, I was still distraught and unable to forget Naren. After a while, Priya and Iyer again had a misunderstanding. I tried to make peace between the two, but Priya Amma decided that it was better to stay away from Iyer. She returned to Switzerland and I went back to Aachen.

I thought about what I should do. I could not do sex work in a room like Priya Amma and Iyer. I wanted a classier job. I discovered a website where one could find rich clients and uploaded new photographs of myself along with my email address. My first client was an elderly man from Switzerland. He emailed me and asked me if I could come to Zurich. He said that he would give me 1,000 francs for every night that I spent with him.

Within minutes of me saying yes, he sent me an air ticket to Zurich. The man was white and must have been about seventy. He was waiting for me at the airport the next day. When he saw me, he said, 'You're very beautiful.'

We drove to his home in his expensive car. Right at the beginning, he paid me 2,000 francs for two nights with him. I spent the day eating and watching television with this man who lived alone. We had sex at night. The money he gave me helped me accept his demands. Until yesterday, men had insulted me for being poor. But today, someone had bought me a plane ticket, paid me thousands of francs and organised a feast for me. I decided that I would no longer take a step back.

There was good news waiting for me the next morning. I had applied for a flight attendant's job at an Arab airline a few days ago. I received an email from the airline asking me to appear for the interview. I wanted to look sophisticated for the interview. The elderly man did not hesitate to fulfil my wish. He took me to expensive stores and bought me nice clothes. After spending the second night with him, I went to Priya Amma's place.

Priya Amma was very happy when she saw me. I gave her 300 francs and sent Naren 200 francs. Although I had grown distant from Naren, I was still concerned about him because of our past intimacy. He was having fun in Chennai and had forgotten me. He would call and express his love only when I sent him money.

I heard from his friend that he was having affairs with other women. I was no longer bothered. I helped him as much as I could because of the love and affection he once had for me. I did not tell Priya Amma that I had sent him money. If she knew, she would berate me. In transwoman society, transwomen who give men money are humiliated.

60. Carnival

The summer carnival was on in Zurich. The main roads of Zurich would be full of people in interesting costumes. Rivers of alcohol would flow through the city accompanied by song and dance. Priya Amma and I went to the carnival in flamboyant clothes and beautiful makeup.

There was a group of drunken white men dancing. As we danced with them, I noticed two Tamil men staring at us. It made me angry. I asked them in German, 'What do you want?' One of them asked, 'Don't you know Tamil?' I told him that I'm from Columbia. The man next to him spoke to me in broken Spanish. I replied in equally bad Spanish, 'Hasn't your mother told you not to stare at women?' I did not know if he understood what I said.

Just then some white men asked me to dance. I walked away. But those Tamil men followed us like monkeys who have spotted toddy. Priya Amma and I decided to go somewhere else to escape them. But when they began to follow us, Priya became scared. I asked her to be brave. As the men neared us, one of them said sorry in German. He asked his friend to apologise as well. This was new. Priya Amma's fear disappeared, and she said, 'We are Tamil too.'

One of the men was called Nakul. As we talked, we realised that we were both the same age. When I told him that my birthday was the next day, he suggested we celebrate it at a bar. We drank late into the night. At midnight, Nakul kissed my lips and wished me a happy birthday.

Priya Amma was delirious. She asked me if we should take them home. But I did not like Nakul's friend. He was a little rough with me, so I said no. We thanked them for their hospitality and left. I expected that Naren would call me at any moment to wish me on my birthday.

I waited all day for Naren to call me. But the call never came. I called him myself that evening. He sounded unenthusiastic to speak to me and did not say anything about my birthday. I asked, 'Do you know that it's my birthday today?' He simply said, 'I forgot.' I immediately hung up. That birthday was like a day of mourning.

Priya Amma and I did not have any money left because we had spent it all at the carnival. Priya called the Horseman. She told him that there were two women waiting for him. The Horseman came soon with a bottle of wine. He paid us 500 francs each.

The Horseman fondled Priya Amma's breasts as he had sex with me. He came in ten minutes, showered and went back to his horse farm. After he was gone, I lay in bed thinking all kinds of things. Priya Amma asked me if I was worried about something. I said no.

'Many men have raped me in the name of love,' I finally said. 'But he paid us for his pleasure and left. This is a clear arrangement. I'm now mature enough to understand that there is a difference between love, lust and sex work. There's nothing to worry about.'

I returned to Germany because I had to prepare for my job interview. The first thing I did after reaching home was to call Naren. I was ready to tell him, 'I hate you. This is the end of our relationship.' But before I could say anything, he began with his usual refrain. He said that his trip to India was not successful and that he would soon return to Canada to make money and then marry me in a formal ceremony.

I took a deep breath and said, 'Sorry, Naren. During the time you had forgotten me, I slept with other men. I'm not the type of woman to cry and fall at the feet of men who have insulted her.' Naren did not believe me. He said, 'Don't fool around, Thanuja. I know I'm the only man you love.'

I sent him a picture of Nakul kissing me. When Naren saw the picture, he began to sob. I heartlessly said, 'That is how I was crying all these days.' I hung up and that was the end of our relationship. I felt heartbroken as well, but it was what I had to do.

61. The Interview

The interview for the flight attendant position was held at a five-star hotel in Cologne. I wore the expensive clothes that were bought for me by my client in Switzerland. They fitted me well. When I arrived for the interview, I noticed that there were many other applicants present.

The competition was tough. The others had graduated from college but I had discontinued my college education. I could not tell the interviewers that. Nor could I let them know that I was a transwoman, as they would use that as a reason to disqualify me. The other candidates would not have faced such difficulties in their lives.

Despite my best efforts, I was rejected in the first round of interviews. Although I was very disappointed, I hardened myself and kept trying. I applied to two other airline companies in Germany and Switzerland. The German airline invited me for an interview.

That interview was held in Frankfurt. There were several exams including those that tested my computer skills and English. I felt confident during the exams. During the interview, they asked me why I didn't complete my education. 'For personal reasons,' I replied.

They said they would inform me of their decision after four weeks. I left feeling hopeful that I would get the job. When I told my family about it, Amma said, 'You'll certainly not get the job.' She tried her best to destroy my hope. Her inauspicious words came true four weeks later.

I joined a WhatsApp group for Malaysian transwomen. I wasted my days chatting with people in the group. I talked to a person who said that she was Iyer Savitri's friend. She told me that Iyer was struggling alone in Cologne, so I went to Cologne to meet Iyer. She was living in the same room as before doing sex work. When she saw me, she hugged me and cried.

Iyer asked me to stay with her. I decided that I would stay with her and do sex work until I got a flight attendant position. I noticed that Iyer was aging rapidly. Germany's fine potatoes, milk and beer had made her put on weight. When they saw me, many of her clients preferred me because I was younger. I earned 500 euros a day. If I worked as a flight attendant, it would take me a week to earn the same amount.

Priya Amma did not like the fact that I was living with her enemy. She asked me to get away from her. But I could not give up on Iyer. Priya and I finally ended up quarrelling. She hurt me and insulted me. 'There's nothing between us anymore,' I said to Priya and ended our friendship. Iyer compensated for Priya Amma's loss.

After spending a week in Cologne, I received an invitation for an interview from a Swiss airline. I was happy and told Iyer that I was going back to Aachen. She saw me off at the railway station and said, 'We will meet again on a plane.'

At home, my father's drinking habit had gotten worse. His love for gambling and the debts he had incurred as a result had led to many mental health issues. He would behave oddly, like suddenly waking up at night and switching off the heat. I would wake up from the cold and switch it on again, but he would switch it off the moment I fell back asleep. There was something that Appa did that I just could not stand. He would come home drunk every night and fight with Amma. She would suffer like a trapped mouse. But when he moved to hit my mother, I would intervene and rescue her. Once, I told him, 'If you hit Amma again, I'll call the police.' Appa was furious and tried to hit me. 'You whore!' he yelled. Amma now tried to intervene. Appa yelled, 'Get out, you son of a whore!' I tried to calm myself by going to my room but then I heard him beat Amma. When I rushed to stop him, he hit me as well. Appa's abuse made me furious and sad. I went back to my room and locked the door. Then I called the police and reported an incident of domestic violence. Five minutes later, the police knocked on our door.

The first thing they did was make Appa leave the house. He was forbidden from entering the house for a week. I do not know whether Appa really learnt anything except that we were not in Sri Lanka but in Europe. His hatred for me doubled.

62. Back to Switzerland

The last time I was in Zurich, I had met a white man called Romano at a bar. He was a fifty-year-old divorcee. I met him at a time when he was trying hard to find a partner. I had saved his phone number just in case. Now I called him and told him that I had an interview in his city.

He was eager to see me again and asked me to stay at his house. He came to receive me at the airport. It was clear that he was attracted to me. But I was not attracted to him. I got in touch with him only because I needed a place to stay in Zurich. His house was in a beautiful village on the outskirts of the city. The house was surrounded by cornfields. It was almost like a farmhouse, with sheep grazing behind the house. I felt that this was the right place to stay.

Romano was born to Italian and Swiss parents. He was a senior officer in the transport department. He took me to an expensive restaurant for dinner. He said that he liked me a lot and tried to seduce me but I did not reciprocate his advances. Once we were back at his home, I went to sleep early because I was exhausted. I woke up in the middle of the night and felt Romano caressing my body. But I kept pretending to be asleep. After some time, I heard him slip away.

No matter how disappointed I was with my transwoman mother, I felt that it was not right to leave Zurich without visiting her. I called Priya and we met at the railway station. After we spoke for a while, our old misunderstandings dissolved like smoke. We were friends again. I spent that night at Priya Amma's. My interview was the following afternoon.

At the interview, there were several exams but they shortlisted just three women for the next round. I was again rejected. I began to feel bitter about life. How much longer would I have to struggle before dying? I called Priya Amma and wept. She consoled me and asked me to come to her place.

Priya Amma said with conviction, 'We'll never find jobs!' She wanted me to become a full-time sex worker. However, I reminded myself that as my 'mother', she knew she would get a share of my earnings!

Her transwoman mothers had extracted their share of her earnings. Now it was Priya Amma's turn to demand her share.

63. The Queen

Priya suggested that we go to a disco and forget our cares. We wore garish makeup and high heels like Hollywood actors and entered a disco catering to wealthy men who were in search of sexual partners. The place was full of sex workers who were mostly women. As we walked through the crowd, no one could tell that we were transwomen. The faces of the other sex workers fell with envy when they saw how long our legs were.

There was a large white man ogling at the women sitting at the table next to ours where we were having our drinks. He looked like a clown in his colourful clothes and football shoes that made him look like a Swiss version of MGR, the Tamil film star. However, we soon found that he was very generous. He politely asked us, 'Can I buy you drinks, ladies?' When we said yes, he began supplying our table with the finest alcohol. I was so happy that I forgot I did not have a job. We drank as much as we could and had more than our share of fun.

The man who showered us with alcohol was called David. He must have been around fifty. He gave me his visiting card, which I carefully kept in my handbag. When David went off to dance in a drunken frenzy, Priya and I left the bar.

It was 3 a.m. when we got back home. Priya hugged me as we lay in bed. 'Don't ever leave me,' she said. 'I suffer a lot without you.' I tightly embraced her. I reminded myself that she had given me the love that

I had not received from my own mother. We dozed off in each other's arms.

I went back to Romano's place that evening because it would only be fair to spend at least a few hours with the man who had given me a place to stay. Romano made a delicious meal for me that night. After dinner, we sat close to each other and watched a movie on television. He made a few boring attempts to draw my attention. But I was not in the least attracted to him.

Finally, he gave me a wad of cash. That got my attention. I put the money away safely and then threw myself on him. We had sex but the sex did not give me any joy. I was mechanical like a veteran sex worker.

However, all the men I had loved had used and discarded me like a sex toy. I was more satisfied with Romano, who had given me money and a place to stay. He did not abuse my body either. He soon came and then I slept in peace.

The next evening, I went to meet Priya Amma. As we were wondering what to do, she suggested that we call David, the generous man we met at the disco the other night. I called him and asked if he wanted to meet. He invited us to an expensive restaurant.

As the three of us were eating, David stupidly said, 'Priya, I prefer your younger sister.' I knew that this would end in conflict. Priya Amma easily became jealous and insecure. Indeed, Priya soon said that she had a headache and went back home. I was conflicted and went to Romano's place that night.

David called me the next afternoon and said, 'Thanuja, I like you a lot. Can we meet?' I agreed. I called Priya Amma and told her that I was going to meet David. Priya did not want us to meet and tried to scare me by saying, 'David belongs to a mafia gang. He'll kidnap you.' It was clear that she was trying to control me.

I replied, 'I want to know what a mafia gang is like. I couldn't become a flight attendant. Let me see if I can at least get a job in a mafia gang.'

David and I met at a café. He was like a child who said whatever came to his mind. He told me that his ex-wife was a wealthy sex worker and they had two daughters. He then said that he was smitten by my dark complexion and asked me if I could spend my weekends with him. That was when my life took a positive turn.

David looked like a clown, but he was actually a magnate. He was a wealthy man who owned a beautiful house in Davos. We met there every weekend. He plied me with wine and gave me a lot of money and I satisfied his needs. I liked this life because I had lots of money.

When I was not with David, I would spend my time with Priya Amma and Romano. I invested the money I was getting in gold jewellery. When Priya Amma noticed that I seemed richer, her jealousy started to emerge like a snake. I made sure to spend a lot of money on her.

David introduced me to his mother and her husband. His mother's name was Evelyn and she lived in a palatial home in Luzern. She was an affectionate woman who really liked me. Evelyn's husband was thirty years younger than her. The four of us went to Paris and stayed at the Shangri-La. It was a luxurious hotel where it cost more than a 1,000 euros a night.

The staff at the hotel treated me like a queen. It was like a dream. I could not understand the changes in my life. I was certainly not in love with David. But I liked the joys and comforts he gave me. I did not know where this journey would end. Soon, David began to fall in love with me. It came to a point where he could no longer live without me.

64. The Cremation Ground

According to myth, Aravan was born to Arjuna and the Naga princess Ulupi. An 'ideal man' needed to be sacrificed to Kali for the Pandavas to win the battle of Kurukshetra. Krishna chose Aravan to be sacrificed. Aravan agreed but he said that he wanted to get married and enjoy a night of conjugal bliss before being sacrificed. But who would marry a man who was going to die the next day?

Krishna assumed the form of Mohini and married Aravan. The next morning, Aravan was sacrificed. His decapitated head participated in the war and vanquished the Kaurava forces. He is called Kuthavandar because he held a knife in his mouth and waged war against the Kauravas.

However, there were actually two sacrifices. Krishna sacrificed himself too. Indian transwomen liken themselves to the female form that Krishna assumed after sacrificing his male body. Therefore, Aravan is their husband. Transwomen turn to myths for the recognition denied to them by civilised society and modern laws.

There is an important ceremony that takes place once a year at a temple in a village called Koovakam near Vizhupuram in India. On a full moon night known as Chitra Purnima, transwomen gather at a temple dedicated to Kuthandavar for a festival. It is not just transwomen from India but also from different parts of the world who dress up like brides and get 'married' by having the priest tie talis around their necks. They sing and dance all night.

The next day there is a chariot festival during which transwomen light lamps and perform the Kummi dance. When Aravan's chariot moves towards the cremation ground, transwomen weep and lament as they follow it. Aravan is sacrificed at noon. Transwomen strip themselves of all the auspicious signs of marriage, sever their talis and become widows.

I had long wanted to attend the festival. I thought my wish would come true this year thanks to David. Also, I was losing hair and I wanted to look for a cure in India. I asked David if I could go on a trip to India. He said that he would pay for it. He told me not to travel such a long distance alone. 'Take your mother with you,' he said and gave me 4,000 francs.

Once I was back home, I asked my mother to go to India with me. I told her that I wanted to find a cure for my hair loss. When she asked me how we would pay for the trip, I told her that I worked at a Swiss restaurant for a couple of months and saved some money. Amma agreed to accompany me on my trip. I was happy and enthusiastic and called Sundari Pati to tell her that I would be attending the festival at Koovakam.

65. Back to Tamil Nadu

When we arrived in Chennai, my aunt's family was at the airport waiting to receive us. They saw me as a woman for the first time. Although they had heard of my transformation, they were astonished to see me. Their driver could not tell that I was a transwoman. It was not just him; most of the people I met in Tamil Nadu did not question my adopted gender. Perhaps it was because my mother was with me nearly all the time. Most people have only seen transwomen alone on the roads and at railway stations. They have perhaps never seen a transwoman with her family.

Although I was drenched in sweat in the scorching heat, Chennai made me happy. This was a lively city. I was excited to see the land that I associated with my childhood. I had idlis and masala dosas to my heart's content. I spent a lot of money on cures for my hair loss. But I was not too bothered by the expense.

Sundari Pati called me and asked me to accompany a transwoman called Mallika who had come to Chennai from Singapore to attend the same temple festival that I was going to. Actually, I already knew Mallika from Facebook. She was a famous Bharatnatyam dancer. I met her at the airport and took her to my aunt's place.

Only then did I inform Amma of my plan to go to the temple festival. She did not object, but she told Mallika, 'My daughter is innocent. You must take care of her.' Amma had finally accepted Thanujan, the fruit of her womb, as her daughter Thanuja.

Mallika was from Kerala. She had learnt Bharatnatyam from Kalakshetra and had been teaching the dance in Singapore. Only after she turned forty did she begin to identify herself as a transwoman. She had been a highly renowned dancer in Singapore, but she lost her reputation when she declared herself a transwoman. Her career as a dancer came to an end and she became a sex worker.

When Mallika and I arrived in Vizhupuram, we found Sundari Pati was already there. She had reserved a room for us in a hotel. We got ready and went to watch the transwoman beauty competition that was called the Miss Koovakam beauty contest. I thought that such a contest was unnecessary. If a transwoman is selected among scores of transwomen as the winner, what about the ones who are not selected? Are they ugly? I do not like contests where several transwomen have to lose just to encourage one of them.

The hall where the contest took place had a festive atmosphere. Compared to the number of transwomen present, there were more lascivious men there to harass them. Some of the attending transwomen had achieved success as writers, actors and social activists. I discovered my dear friend Angel in the crowd and embraced her. Angel stayed with me that night.

The next morning, there were transwomen all around the village and its neighbouring areas. It was the day when the transwomen would receive their talis from Aravan. We dressed up like brides and went to the temple. Several transwomen like to pretend that the priest's hands are Aravan's hands when they receive their talis. I did not want a tali because I believed David was like my husband. I did not want to sever the tali either.

At night, Koovakam glowed with transwomen like Indra's heaven. The songs and dancing got us excited. There were plenty of boorish men around with lust in their eyes and violence on their minds. The transwomen were distressed by their harassment. A few men even got together and carried some transwomen away to rape them. The police were unable to prevent these crimes.

During a later visit to this village, I was filmed driving these lecherous men away and became famous on the internet when that clip was included in a documentary made by a north Indian journalist. The video had more than a million views and was crucial in making me better known to the public.

We reached the cremation ground at noon the day after receiving the tali. There were thousands of transwomen in saris they had worn the previous day with talis around their necks. When Aravan majestically entered on a chariot only to be broken and sacrificed, the cries of the transwomen were heartbreaking. The talis we had worn the previous day were severed and our bangles broken. We assumed the appearance of widows in white saris as we grieved.

We returned to our hotel with heavy hearts. That night, I was the subject of a dispute. Sundari Pati had decided to sever my ties with Priya Amma and make me Tilakam Pati's daughter. However, Tilakam Pati was Priya's mother, so I would become Priya's younger sister according to the jamaat's new resolution.

I did not want to become Tilakam Pati's daughter. She was only interested in money and showed no love or concern for anybody. But I could not go against the jamaat's decision. I immediately called Priya and informed her of the jamaat's decision. She refused to accept this decision and fought with me.

When Sundari Pati intervened, the fight grew bigger. I discovered from their fight that they had several problems and had exchanged a lot of money. I also learnt that Priya had falsely accused me of many things and was spreading rumours among the transwomen about me.

I was exhausted with the jamaat's fights and disputes. The next morning, I went back to Chennai feeling anxious. Angel and I walked about the streets of Chennai shopping and trying on new clothes. We bought the same clothes and dressed up like twin stars and enlivened the streets of Chennai. When it was time to return to Germany, Angel saw us off at the airport. I heard that Angel later moved to Canada.

66. Mentors

After we reached Germany, I stayed at home for just a day before going to Zurich. This time I avoided staying at Priya's place and stayed with Romano instead. The only problem with that arrangement was that Romano could not keep his hands off me. But at least he would not hurt me like Priya could.

I met David that evening. He had just returned from a trip to Dubai with his two daughters. The expensive gold bangles from Dubai that he presented to me suggested that he had been longing for me and had been unhappy without me. I divided my time between David and Romano and accumulated a lot of money.

Soon, I could buy gold bangles for my mother. My family began to respect me. Appa began to tolerate me. I travelled with David and we visited many countries together. My ex-mother Priya could not stand any of this. The venomous serpent of jealousy emerged from her heart. She called David and said, 'Your lover Thanuja is a transwoman.'

My life collapsed in a day. David left me. I knew Priya was jealous of me but never in my wildest dreams did I think that she would betray me like this. My humiliation and sorrow turned into anger. I went in search of Priya and cursed her. 'You'll be destroyed,' I yelled. Priya wept and asked me to forgive her. Her tears may have been genuine but they failed to move me.

If I pleasured Romano at night, he would pay me. But his money was not enough for me. I was used to a luxurious life like the kind David and I had been living. I wanted elaborate feasts, dance performances and the finest alcohol. I liked wearing expensive and well-made clothes. All I could think of was having a lot of money and spending it.

I stayed with Romano and looked for a job, but I could not find one. However, there were plenty of clients for sex work. They were everywhere in the streets, on trains, in bars and even in temples. Just as

I was thinking of becoming a full-time sex worker, I met a university professor named Selina Prufrock who was doing research on Tamil transwomen who live in Europe.

Selina was a Swiss national and was introduced to me through a German transwoman. I found her to be a very loving person. She cried when she heard my life story. The tears that others shed for us cannot be found in rivers or even in the Zamzam Well.

My conversations with Selina gradually transformed me. She made me feel self-confident. I adopted her as my mentor. Selina encouraged me to complete my college studies and graduate. She said that I should work towards the well-being of the transwomen community. Because of her, I could see that no matter how far I had travelled along the wrong path, I could still return. I buried my desire for money and a lavish lifestyle and went back home.

My family was truly happy when I told them that I would resume my studies. Then I got a call from Kamini Chithi, who wanted to meet me. She told me that she had gone to Malaysia and married a Tamil man there. She was now back in Germany. I thought that I needed a true transwoman mother who would love me. I immediately went to see Kamini.

She and I were meeting after a long time. I told her about all my loves, betrayals and disappointments. She held my face in her hands and comforted me. Then I touched her feet and said, 'Please accept me as your daughter.' Kamini accepted my request with joy. She said that she would talk to Sundari Pati about adopting me. We decided that we would go to Malaysia together and perform all the necessary rituals to become mother and daughter. I went home feeling joyous.

I became friends on Facebook with Para, who said that he was a Tamil Canadian actor. He did not know that I was a transwoman and I could tell that he was interested in me by the number of messages he sent me on Facebook every day. He often asked me to visit him in Canada.

I thought I had had enough of men living in Canada and declined his offer. When I was chatting with Para, I told him I went to Malaysia which got him excited. He asked me to accompany him to Sri Lanka and Malaysia during the holidays. He said that he would buy me a return ticket from Germany to Malaysia via Sri Lanka. It had been fifteen years since I had left Sri Lanka. I longed to go back to my motherland. I accepted his invitation with joy.

67. The Motherland

Para was waiting for me at the Colombo airport. He looked unkempt. He took me to a hotel by the beach. He was as much in a hurry to have sex as he was to express his love and asked me for sex as soon as we entered the room. I was ready after I had drunk half a bottle of wine.

Para had brought me clothes and perfumes from Canada. He uttered drunken words of love, but he did not bother me otherwise. He spent all day asking me not to let go of him. He truly was a loving man. As if I did not know how far this love would go! I no longer had any infatuation or desire for men. Time had dissolved my desire and my tears had washed away my lust for men. I was no longer prepared to sacrifice my self-respect at the feet of men in the name of love.

The next day, Para went out for some work. I remembered that Sara, whom I had met in Thailand when I went to get my breasts enlarged, lived in Colombo. I called her and spent that morning with her family. When I returned to the hotel that night, Para was waiting for me and looked distressed. He uttered the same old romantic words but all he felt was lust.

Para and I travelled through southern Sri Lanka. I spent my days on the beach and in the lush forests. Para then went to Trincomalee to visit his in-laws. As I could not go with him, I stayed with Sara. Her family showered me with love. I told Sara that I really wanted to go to Yazhpanam. She agreed to accompany me.

When I set foot in Yazhpanam, I took some soil and smeared it on my forehead. The scars of war could still be seen not just in the landscape but also on the faces of the people. When I went to visit my relatives in Mankumban and Velanai, they did not ostracise me and instead welcomed me. I think my gender did not matter to them because I had come from abroad. God knows what they said behind my back!

When I was staying at my mama's place at Velanai, Vinu Mama called me. You probably remember him. He was the uncle who would beat me when I was a small boy fifteen years ago because he could not tolerate my effeminacy. Now he was my Facebook friend. He asked me to meet him when I returned to Colombo. I wanted to see him too because I wanted to appear as a complete woman before the uncle who had tortured me for my nascent effeminacy.

After spending three days in Yazhpanam, I returned to Colombo. Vinu Mama sent a car to Sara's place to pick me up. I bid farewell to Sara and her family. The car took me to a hotel by the beach. I found it amusing that it was the same hotel I had stayed in with Para just a few days ago. Vinu Mama was waiting for me in one of the rooms.

I remembered Vinu Mama as a majestic man. But he now appeared shorter than me and had grown emaciated. When he hugged me, his hands were trembling. He had hooked nails that had grown yellow. He could not have been more than forty, but alcohol had ruined his health. He had brought some special Sri Lankan toddy with him. We chatted as we drank it. We found that we had endless stories to share.

Finally, I asked him why he always beat me in those days. 'What was the point of beating you?' he said with a scowl of disapproval. 'You've anyway become a woman.' With the same scowl he suddenly leaned forward. I thought he was going to scold me when the scoundrel kissed my lips. I was shocked as if a snake had bitten me on my mouth. Is this what you call familial love? Is this what you call Tamil culture?

My uncle mistook my astonishment for coyness. He said, 'You live abroad and yet you're so shy …' I was prepared to let him know that I was not shy. I grabbed his head and gave him a French kiss. We had sex. It was my way of telling him that in spite of all his beatings and attempts to control me, I valued my own emotions and became a woman. I achieved what my soul wanted.

No one can even imagine what happens in a transwoman's life. You cannot understand us with mainstream norms, laws, culture, literature and principles. We have been betrayed by history and our journey is a perplexing circular path. No one has been able to undo this knot, not even ourselves.

68. Menstruation

Tamils use the term *'tirunambi'* to refer to those who were born with female bodies but became men. Kamini had a brother who was a tirunambi. His name was Satya. When I went to Malaysia, he was waiting for me at the Kuala Lumpur airport. Satya was the first Tamil tirunambi I met. We instantly became good friends.

I really liked Satya because he was very sweet. We went to Kamini's home, which was in a place called Johor Bahru. She lived in a large house surrounded by natural beauty. She lovingly embraced me and I took her blessings by touching her feet. She was the head of the household and lived with her husband, her brother and ten other transwomen.

With the others as witnesses, I was formally adopted by Kamini. I acquired new relationships through the ritual and now had ten transwomen sisters and nieces. Half of them were sex workers while the other half worked at stores in Singapore. They made more money in Singapore than in Malaysia and lived comfortable lives.

One of my new sisters was Kamali. She had just undergone her gender reassignment surgery. Kamini decided to perform a grand ceremony for her. Although I had my nirvanam done five years ago, no one performed an adoption ceremony for me. I asked Kamini to perform the ceremony for me, and she agreed. Now I was going to blossom into a complete woman according to transwoman tradition.

I have danced on stages when I was young and sang, 'You need to menstruate to be a woman.' I had to do penance in this life to become a woman. My penance has borne fruit because of Kamini. On an auspicious day in the month of Masi in 2017, a ceremony was performed for Kamali and me in the presence of more than a hundred transwomen.

I stood there like a bride dressed in all the clothes and finery that I had always desired as a child, bearing all the auspicious signs including a garland and flowers in my hair. I was amazed to see myself in the mirror. When I was young, my imaginary friends would be standing on either side dressed like I was now.

I seriously re-examined my life during my time in Malaysia. I had thousands of questions about the future. Over there I met transwomen who did sex work when they were young and were abandoned and lay on the streets when they grew old. I thought about transwomen like Sheela, who lived in Europe with mental illness.

I also learnt lessons from the transwomen who live in India without any basic rights as well as the transwomen who are forced to live secret lives in Yazhpanam. I decided that whether I was going to suffer or succeed was in my hands. What would I have to do once I returned to Germany? Who were my true friends? What were my responsibilities?

I had found clear answers to these questions. I must study well and find a job that will let me live life with self-respect. My true friends were the transwomen community. My primary responsibility was to strive for the transwomen community's progress.

I resumed my studies and looked for part-time jobs at hospitals. I learnt to live a frugal life with the little money that I earned from my jobs and the government scholarship I was receiving. I rented a small room in Düsseldorf and lived alone. It was the same city where I once looked for men who drank and partied.

In April 2018, I attended my sister's wedding in Switzerland. At the wedding, my family and relatives accepted me as a woman. I had to be firm and continuously struggle to change their minds. We will have to continue our struggle until the world treats transwomen as equals. We do not hate anyone. There is no legitimate reason for the world to hate and exclude us.

I am always in touch with my mentor, Selina Prufrock. I help her with her research on transwomen. I collaborate with organisations that fight for the rights of the LGBTQIA+ community. Eventually, I was awarded the 'Born to Win' award for my small efforts to create awareness in the transwomen community.

Selina occasionally organises talks on transwomen at Swiss universities. Once, her students requested me to write about my life at one of these events. They were the ones who inspired me to write my autobiography. Ever since I began to write it, I no longer look for my imaginary friends.

Instead of telling them, I have told you my story without concealing anything. I trust you have not just used your mind when reading this book. I hope you also read it with your soul.

Translator's Afterword

I was asked by a friend to write an essay on queer literature in Tamil for a volume that he was co-editing. As I looked for texts, I discovered that there were no significant works on queerness in Tamil. Some of the novels and short stories I found were not finely crafted and reinforced gender stereotypes by conflating gender with sexuality. They were sentimental in their portrayal of queer characters, who were often reduced to tragic victims.

The dearth of scholarship on queer literature in Tamil pre-empts the possibility of identifying queer texts and formal and aesthetic concerns across these texts. However, there have been quite a few significant memoirs and autobiographies in Tamil by transwomen that are honest and evocative portrayals of their lives. These accounts do not sensationalise the suffering that they experience.

M. Kannan, an independent scholar at the French Institute of Pondicherry, introduced me to Thanuja Singam's eponymous autobiography. The essay I ended up writing was a comparative study of *Thanuja* and A. Revathi's autobiography, *The Truth about Me: A Hijra Life Story* (2010). I was struck by how both these autobiographies embodied negotiations with gendered and sexual norms that are spatially organised and reinforced: toilets, homes, trains, hijra households and neighbourhoods.

The 2010s have been a crucial decade in the history of queer discourse in India with the emergence of a whole spectrum of queer voices that have demanded justice in the face of homophobia and gendered forms of oppression. In the 2014 *National Legal Services Authority vs Union of India* judgement, the Supreme Court of India passed a landmark ruling that upheld the right of all people to self-identify their gender. It was the first judgement to acknowledge the third gender or transgender people.

Then, in 2017, the Supreme Court ruled that the Right to Privacy was a fundamental right, a ruling that was important for the protection of sexual orientation and which came as a relief to the LGBTQA+ community. The Supreme Court further decriminalised consensual sexual acts between adults irrespective of their gender in the 2018 *Navtej Singh Johar vs Union of India* judgement.

Transgender people, activists, students and lawyers protested against the Transgender Persons (Protection of Rights) Bill that was passed in 2018 because it was seen as regressive and violated the 2014 Supreme Court judgement. Under the 2018 bill, begging was criminalised, which would affect the lives of certain sections of the transgender population. Also, transgender children were barred from being separated from their families.

But the central objection against the 2018 judgement was its failure to recognise a transgender person's right to self-identification; identification of transgender people would be done by a district screening committee. The bill made gender reassignment surgery a prerequisite for those who wished to transition from one gender to another.

In addition, it did not grant backward-class status to the transgender community as the court had proposed and also abolished national and state commissions for transgender people and transgender rights courts as well as reservations for transgender individuals in official appointments. The demand for self-identification and the recognition of transgender rights is thus an ongoing struggle.

In their chronological volume *Same-Sex Love in India* (2008), Ruth Vanita and Salim Kidwai bring together queer texts that span the literary history of India, from puranic texts and kavyas to Bhakti and Urdu poetry. There is a focus on the ghazal form and on modern short stories and poems. One of the main aims of the book is to dismiss the myth that homosexuality is a Western import.

Based on their readings of these texts, Vanita and Kidwai propose a few tropes through which same-sex relations can be imagined and understood in all their fluidity: friendship as a model of same-sex intimacy and homoeroticism; switching genders over multiple lives to serve as a (retrospective) justification of same-sex love; and gender change, especially in gods (for example, Vishnu), which permits the possibility of cross-gender intimacy. These tropes are suggestive of the uneasy correlation of sexuality to gender or queer and transgender identities.

The writer Devdutt Pattanaik's work on Hindu mythology suggests that there are ample instances of characters from the puranas that cross-dress or transition between genders. Some characters lead celibate lives even as they enjoy deeply erotic same-sex friendships. But it is important not to assume that the pre-colonial period was a period of sexual licence and freedom—it was an era characterised by different moral perceptions and hierarchies that became criminalised and punished under colonial law.

Homosexuality, for instance, was a punishable offence according to the *Arthashastra* but it was not considered as egregious as robbing a young woman or girl of her virginity or indulging in bestiality. But in the colonial period, the homosexual emerged as an aberrant person who was reduced to his or her sexuality. Queer sexuality was seen as something to be regulated lest it became a threat to colonial masculinity and power.

In *For the Record* (2009), Anjali Arondekar draws attention to the anxiety that queerness elicited and the colonial state's determination to regulate non-normative forms of sexuality. The nationalist rhetoric of the postcolonial state reproduced the homophobia of the colonials and looked to regulate or even eliminate sexual irregularities, which were seen as antithetical to the progress of the new nation. Unlike the pre-modern and early modern world, where same-sex intimacies among men enjoyed greater visibility, the colonial and postcolonial period witnessed a greater representation of female homoeroticism.

The early decades of the twenty-first century witnessed the emergence of many new transgender voices in India in the form of autobiographies, memoirs, online and television interviews, videos, political protests and agitations. These forms of expression sought to draw attention to the social and political disenfranchisement of transgender people and their desire for equality and freedom.

Some of the earliest trans autobiographies in Indian languages were published in the 2010s and translated into English. Among them is A. Revathi's *The Truth about Me: A Hijra Life Story*, which was first published as a translation in English and only then in the original Tamil four years later in 2014. The second part of Revathi's autobiography, *A Life in Transactivism* (2016), describes her life as a transactivist and her nurturing relationship with transmen.

Also published at this time was Living Smile Vidya's *I Am Vidya* (2013). Written in Tamil, the book describes her challenges as a transwoman and her struggle to transition. It was followed by memoirs from Laxmi Narayan Tripathi, whose *Me Hijra, Me Laxmi* (2015) and *Red Lipstick* (2016), originally published in Marathi, describe her intimate and creative relationship with music and dance and her engagement with activism.

Other notable works in the genre from this period are Manobi Bandyopadhyay's *A Gift of Goddess Lakshmi* (2017), which was published in Bengali and describes the life of India's first transgender college principal; Kalki Subramaniam's *We Are Not the Others* (2021), a collection of poems, images and articles published in English that captures the stigmatised and marginalised lives of transgender people and their desire for equal rights; Akkai Padmashali's *A Small Step in a Long Journey* (2023), which was published in Kannada and traces her journey from an outcaste sex worker to an activist who, like Revathi, worked for Sangama, an LGBTQA+ group based in Bangalore; and most recently B. Manjamma Jogathi's *From Manjunath to Manjamma* (2023), which was published in Kannada and talks about her life as a traditional folk performer from northern Karnataka.

Thanuja's autobiography, *Thanuja,* was first published in Tamil in 2021. It traces the life of a Sri Lankan Tamil transwoman, or *thirunangai,* whose family migrates to Germany towards the end of the civil war in Sri Lanka. Although most of the autobiography is set in Germany and its neighbouring countries, what is remarkable is that it largely captures an international Tamil-speaking diaspora through the lenses of family, caste and the internet.

In contrast, Revathi spends all her life in India and her autobiography traces her peripatetic life in the 1980s and 1990s—a life of violence and exploitation. She is torn between her hostile family and the hijra community that she belongs to. Her book describes the intimate albeit exploitative ties between 'mothers' and 'daughters' as well as gurus and followers in that community.

Thanuja's family settles in Aachen, where there are other Sri Lankan Tamil families from Jaffna like them. The Tamil world is a small and close-knit one and most of the men that Thanuja dates are second-generation Tamil men living in Europe. Thanuja has access to education and the internet, which opens up a new world of information and intimacy.

Compared to Revathi, Thanuja has an equally fraught but more flexible relationship with the larger hijra community because she, like Laxmi Tripathi and Kalki Subramaniam, is educated and qualified and has a family that becomes supportive of her choices. Laxmi, in particular, is from a more privileged upper-caste background. However, even that does not guarantee social immunity from violence and humiliation. In her book, Laxmi talks about the journey she and her fellow transwomen took from humiliation and stigma to a growing political consciousness that is often expressed in the form of art and activism.

Notwithstanding these differences, many of these autobiographies end on a note of solidarity with the larger transwoman community. The mission of Thanuja's life is to create awareness and fight for the rights of the transwoman and hijra community. Although Thanuja has her differences with some of the transwomen she meets—including her transwoman 'mother' Priya and some of the elders of the community—she needs their emotional support when she is betrayed and exploited by the men she loves. Thanuja's autobiography shares certain themes that resonate with all the aforementioned autobiographies.

First, the early years of every transwoman's life are a significant time during which the transwoman explores her own femininity and enjoys the freedom—often for the first and last time—to enact her femininity without necessarily incurring social censure. This is certainly true of Revathi and Thanuja, both of whom explore their feminine sides by doing certain forms of household work and having intimate relationships with their mothers and female relatives.

Music and dance are crucial forms of self-expression for many transwomen. However, the public performance of femininity also runs the risk of ridicule and violence. There are physical and virtual spaces—such as theatre, temple festivals, cinema (particularly movie songs), social media and online video chats—that represent the possibility of embodying a feminine aesthetic while at the same time negotiating censure, violence and stigma (at least for as long as they are on stage).

Although these expressions of femininity may seem ritualistic and normative to some (Revathi and Thanuja acknowledge this themselves), they are often the only available forms of expression especially for small-town transwomen who belong to a certain generation, caste or class. Their autobiographies often trace their journeys from small towns to cities, where they are exposed to violence, exploitation and poverty. Cities are also where they find support in the form of non-governmental organisations and other politically conscious (and often English-speaking) queer groups.

Second, childhood is often a period of conflict during which the transwoman is not sure whether she is a gay man or a woman who is trapped in a man's body and desires other men (there may also be instances of transwomen who desire other trans or ciswomen). This dilemma is common to Revathi, Thanuja and Laxmi Tripathi's early life.

Third, another important aspect that characterises the childhood and adolescence of many of these transwomen is child sexual abuse. Revathi, Thanuja and Laxmi recount their early experiences of sexual abuse at the hands of strangers and male relatives. They wonder if the effeminacy of their former life as boys is responsible for drawing male attention. Many of them are molested and raped, which makes their femininity an ambivalent source of suffering and self-affirmation.

Thanuja and Laxmi's childhoods are similar in the ways they negotiate male and female spaces by playing sports with the boys on one hand and playing dress-up with the girls on the other. While Revathi and Thanuja are more militant in their self-expressions as transwomen, Laxmi does not wish to reduce herself to a transgender person and simultaneously inhabits other genders and worlds.

Laxmi leads a double life. In one, she secretly works as a bar dancer. However, she refuses to have sex with her customers or become a sex worker to support her family. When she is not dancing or with her fellow hijras, she leads her other life in which she dresses in men's clothes and presents herself as a responsible son to her supportive parents. She does not want to be ghettoised and even her guru tells her that it is not compulsory to wear a sari all the time.

But like Thanuja, Revathi and many other transwomen, Laxmi soon understands that the hijra community is quite conservative and exploitative. She realises that she does not fully belong either to the hijra world or the non-hijra world. She feels all the more invisible because she has not undergone sex-change surgery and has no 'proof' of being a transwoman.

The very act of writing is fundamental to the construction of an autobiographical self that is based on one's memory of the past. This autobiographical self is contingent on its experience of time and space and is always in the making. In the case of transgender autobiographies, writing is a testimony to the author's embodied sense of gender dysphoria. It incurs censure and humiliation and becomes a source of self-affirmation that enables the author to negotiate and potentially overcome the painful feeling of exclusion.

For many of these transwomen, language and writing become conduits to a place where the structural exclusions that constitute gender norms are both reinforced and undermined. In Thanuja's case, she is humiliated and beaten by her father and brother for being effeminate. Many of the Tamil men she encounters humiliate her for being effeminate even as they secretly desire her. Thanuja also draws attention to the lies and hypocrisies that constitute dominant forms of masculinity.

Thanuja's father is a violent drunk who assaults her mother and appropriates her savings. Similarly, there are a number of men who violate Thanuja and exploit her for her money all in the name of love. Dating Tamil men is perceived as a threat to her family's reputation in a close-knit European Tamil diaspora. She is shamed and rejected by one of the Tamil men she loves when his parents discover that she is a transwoman.

The desire to come out as a transwoman is an ever-present challenge for Thanuja, who risks losing everything: her dignity, the men she loves and possibly even her life. However, it is the only way of asserting and seeking legal recognition of her selfhood. She is reluctant to let go of some of the men she dates even though they abuse and exploit her because they validate her femininity and accept her as a woman. Some of the transwomen elders in her community shame her for giving money to men who exploit her, but it does not undermine her determination to work towards the advancement of her community.

Thanuja struggles to procure government documents that would allow her to have legal recognition of her adopted feminine name and gender identity. However, as she finds out, legal recognition does not automatically translate into social acceptance. Thanuja's autobiography stands apart from the other aforementioned autobiographies because of her complex relationship with her own gender and citizenship.

Thanuja's autobiography is written in a fairly simple and standard language that—notwithstanding the use of a few Sri Lankan Tamil words—is intelligible to the average Tamil reader. The challenge for me as a translator was finding—and in some cases even coining—English phrases and idioms that would capture certain culturally specific sayings and proverbs that cannot be adequately conveyed in English. Sometimes the brevity of Tamil expressions would not make sense to the English reader without the use of an explicatory phrase.

Thanuja is a moving and powerful testament to a transwoman's courage and determination to live a life of dignity and self-respect—a life that is ultimately dedicated to the betterment of the transgender community.

References

Anjali Arondekar, *For the Record: On Sexuality and the Colonial Archive in India* (Duke University Press, 2009).

Manobi Bandopadhyay, *A Gift of Goddess Lakshmi*, translated by Jhimli Mukherjee Pandey (Penguin Random House India, 2017).

Rohit K. Dasgupta, 'Queer Sexuality: A Cultural Narrative of India's Historical Archive' in *Rupkatha Journal on Interdisciplinary Studies in Humanities*, Vol. 3, No. 4 (2011).

Manjamma Jogathi, *From Manjunath to Manjamma: The Inspiring Life of a Transgender Folk Artist*, translated by Harsha Bhatt (HarperCollins India, 2023).

Nivedita Menon, *Sexualities* (Women Unlimited, 2007).

Akkai Padmashali, *A Small Step in a Long Journey*, transcribed by Gowri Vijayakumar (Zubaan, 2023).

Devdutt Pattanaik, *Shikhandi and Other Queer Tales They Don't Tell You* (Zubaan, 2014).

—, *The Pregnant King: A Novel* (Penguin, 2014).

Jyoti Puri, *Woman, Body, Desire in Postcolonial India: Narratives of Gender and Sexuality* (Routledge, 1999).

Mrinalini Sinha, *Colonial Masculinity: The 'Manly Englishman' and the 'Effeminate Bengali' in the Late Nineteenth Century* (Manchester University Press, 1995).

Kalki Subramaniam, *We Are Not the Others: Reflections of a Transgender Artivist* (Notion Press, 2021).

A. Revathi, *The Truth about Me: A Hijra Life Story*, translated by V. Geetha (Penguin India, 2010).

—, *A Life in Transactivism*, translated by Nandini Murali (Zubaan, 2016).

T. Singam, *Thanuja: Oru Eezha Thirunangaiyin Payanamum Porattamum* (Karuppu Piradhigal, 2020).

Laxmi N. Tripathi, *Me Hijra, Me Laxmi*, translated by R. Raj Rao and P.G. Joshi (Oxford University Press, 2015).

—, *Red Lipstick: The Men in My Life*, translated by Pooja Pande (Penguin, 2016).

Ruth Vanita and Salim Kidwai, *Same-Sex Love in India: Readings from Literature and History* (Palgrave Macmillan, 2001).

Living S. Vidya, *I Am Vidya: A Transgender's Journey*, translated by V. Ramnarayan (Rupa, 2013).

Translator's Acknowledgements

Let me begin by thanking M. Kannan (French Institute of Pondicherry) for introducing me to this autobiography. I would like to thank Arnab Karmakar for suggesting that I send this translation to Sivapriya. My heartfelt thanks to Tapojay Mandal whose comments and suggestions have made this translation coherent and readable. I wish to thank Megha Arora for her sincere efforts. I am deeply grateful to Thanuja Singam for writing such an honest and moving book which I am sure will be a source of inspiration to the transgender community. I thank my colleagues, my parents and my brother for their unstinting love and support. Lastly, I wish to thank Sivapriya for her invaluable comments and suggestions that have made this translation possible.

About the Author

Thanuja is a dental hygienist in Düsseldorf committed to advancing her education with plans to further her studies in healthcare management. However, her true passion lies beyond the walls of academia and dental practice. She has dedicated herself to activism focusing on the LGBTQIA+ community, a cause close to her heart. Through social media, she has built a platform to amplify voices, spread awareness and foster understanding and acceptance. With over a million followers on TikTok, 220,000 subscribers on YouTube and substantial followings on Instagram, Facebook and other platforms, she has been able to reach and impact countless lives. Her work has not gone unnoticed; she was honoured with YouTube's Silver Button, a testament to the growing acceptance and support for the LGBTQIA+ community.

Thanuja's activism is not just about raising awareness, it's about building a community, a family where LGBTQIA+ individuals, particularly the younger generation, can find support, acceptance and the strength to live authentically without shame.

Thanuja's memoir is an honest and open account of the joys and struggles she has faced as a member of the LGBTQIA+ community. She hopes that through her story readers will gain a deeper understanding of what it means to live as someone like her—someone who has faced adversity but continues to fight for acceptance and equality.

About the Translator

Kiran Keshavamurthy is an assistant professor of English at the Department of Humanities and Social Sciences, IIT Guwahati. He is a scholar of modern Tamil literature and the author of *Beyond Desire: Sexuality in Modern Tamil Literature* (OUP India, 2016). He has written articles and essays on various Tamil writers.